WORKING WIVES
AND
DUAL-EARNER FAMILIES

Working Wives
and
Dual-Earner Families

Rose M. Rubin & Bobye J. Riney

PRAEGER

Westport, Connecticut
London

Library of Congress Cataloging-in-Publication Data

Rubin, Rose M.
    Working wives and dual-earner families / Rose M. Rubin and Bobye J.
Riney.
        p.   cm.
    Includes bibliographical references and indexes.
    ISBN 0–275–94682–7 (alk. paper)
    1. Dual-career families—United States.   I. Riney, Bobye J.
    II. Title.
    HQ536.R83   1994
    306.872—dc20   93–5441

British Library Cataloguing in Publication Data is available.

Library of Congress Catalog Card Number: 93–5441
ISBN: 0–275–94682–7

First published in 1994

Praeger Publishers, 88 Post Road West, Westport, CT 06881
An imprint of Greenwood Publishing Group, Inc.

Printed in the United States of America

The paper used in this book complies with the
Permanent Paper Standard issued by the National
Information Standards Organization (Z39.48–1984).

10 9 8 7 6 5 4 3 2 1

Contents

Figures and Tables

Preface

Debate, including consciousness raising, has flourished and much has been written about the changing roles of men and women and women's increased labor force participation. However, little of this has centered specifically on husbands and wives and the effects of these socioeconomic changes on married-couple families. The objective of this book is to fill this gap with descriptive and empirical research on the economics of dual-earner families and their central role in the economy and society.

The study of dual-earner families has been of special interest to the authors for several years. This topic combines concerns for social welfare, the economic status of families, and numerous public policy issues that will have increasing importance through the 1990s. The United States has already witnessed some concern at the national policy level regarding child care, parental leave, equitable tax status for differing households, and related family issues. This text provides substantive input to ongoing dialogues about these issues that we believe will be helpful to researchers, students, decision makers, and those concerned about the welfare of families.

We want to thank those who have read the manuscript at various stages of development and have made valuable suggestions for its improvement. In particular, we acknowledge the generous encouragement and help of former professors and mentors. Carolyn Bell, professor emeritus, Wellesley College, gave us detailed feedback and important suggestions for broadening the scope of the manuscript. Her comprehensive knowledge and contributions to the literature provided both additional references and innovative perspective on our work. We are truly grateful for her extensive and thoughtful contributions. We are also heavily indebted to Alice Milner, professor emeritus, Texas Woman's University, and Sarah Manning, professor (retired), Purdue University and Buffalo State College, for their detailed editorial comments and suggestions.

David Molina, associate professor in the Department of Economics at the University of North Texas, made major contributions to this project. He was a coauthor of material presented in Chapter 6, which was published in *Journal of Consumer Research*, and in Chapter 7, which was in an unpublished paper presented at the 1990 Western Economics Association meeting in San Diego. We express our thanks for his econometric expertise and assistance.

In addition, we acknowledge the technical assistance of several graduate research assistants: Pornpun Waitayangkoon, Roger Speas, and Ajay Babar. Their help with data analyses, literature search, and preparation of graphic materials is appreciated. Howard Hayghe, of the Bureau of Labor Statistics, was most helpful in providing unpublished data on marital and family characteristics of the labor force.

Without the contributions of each of the above, the book would have had many more deficiencies. We of course take full responsibility for the contents.

We have benefited from the ongoing support of the University of North Texas. In particular, we would like to thank the administrators and faculty colleagues in our academic departments for their encouragement and support. This project was supported in part by several faculty research grants, which facilitated our research.

Last, we wish to acknowledge and thank our families for their continuous support and encouragement.

WORKING WIVES
AND
DUAL-EARNER FAMILIES

1

The Economics of
Dual-Earner Families

The continuing entry of women into the workplace and their labor force attachment are among the most important social and economic trends of the twentieth century. Since 1890 there has been a steady increase of women, including wives, in the labor force as a result of the shift from agricultural to market employment. More recently, wives and mothers have entered the labor force in record numbers and demonstrated remarkable staying power, thus making the economics of dual-earner families a major issue. Although working wives have substantially affected the income, taxes, expenditures, assets, and income distribution of families, research has lagged on the extent of these impacts.

Economic issues of dual-earner families are of interest to researchers, policymakers, and families, but no single text has comprehensively analyzed the effects of labor force participation of married women on the economic status of households. This book fills that void by providing a historical perspective and presenting the findings of empirical research on the economic impacts of wives' work status. Most previous studies do not distinguish the work status of employed wives. The empirical chapters of this text present comparative analyses of the economics of three types of married-couple families, in which the wife is employed full-time or part-time or is not gainfully employed. Because most employed husbands work full-time, we do not make a comparable distinction for husbands and our analyses use full-time employed husbands. We emphasize the period beginning in the early 1970s, when real income growth declined and increased numbers of wives continued to enter the labor force.

The topics on dual-earner families addressed in the following chapters include an overview of their status, the changing impacts of federal income taxes, their costs of having two earners rather than one, their allocation of expenditures, their income and assets, and their effect on the inequality of income distribution. Several of these analyses compare dual-earner with husband-only-earner married-couple families, and some also distinguish among full-time and part-time working-wife families compared with nonemployed-wife households. Throughout the book, reference to one-earner families indicates a husband-only-earner.

BACKGROUND

The unparalleled rise in women's labor force participation has had far-reaching implications for families and for society. After an extended period of economic growth, wages in general stagnated after 1973 and concurrently wives' employment grew substantially. During this period, the increasing prevalence of two-earner families was the factor that maintained the level of average household income. Significant increases in the number and share of dual-income families occurred, as labor force participation of wives expanded even more rapidly than that of other groups of women. The dual-earner family is now more prevalent than the one-earner, with husband and wife employed in almost 60 percent of all married-couple families. Only 17 percent of married couples are one-earner, with the rest having other or no earners.

Changes in the employment status of wives affected the financial resources of dual-earner married couples compared with other households. In 1990, the median income of dual-earner families was 55 percent higher than when only the husband worked: $46,777 compared with $30,265 (U.S. Bureau of the Census 1992). In general, dual-earner families are younger and better educated, have fewer children, and have higher total incomes than one-earner families.

Although dual-earner family income is higher than one-earner income, researchers (Lazear and Michael 1980; Michael 1985) have found that dual-earners do not appear to have a much higher standard of living. This is primarily due to the high costs related to wives' employment and increased taxes. Living standards may be viewed as having two components, purchased goods and services and production within the home. Recognizing that wives still make the major contribution to within-household production and its significant importance to family living standards, our research focuses on wives' market interaction and their financial contributions to the family. Wives' contribution to the household production function is, however, indirectly recognized in the examination of home-production opportunity costs of their employment.

The growth of the two-earner family emphasizes the importance of the household as the unit of analysis in studies of the distribution of income. It also indicates that family earnings may be a more appropriate index of well-being than individual measures of income (Smith 1979). The transformation in work roles raises important issues for family employment decisions, such as the opportunity costs and tax impacts of having two earners, comparative household expenditures, comparative income and assets, and the effect of dual-earners on the distribution of income. Our detailed studies of these questions employ data from the Consumer Expenditure Surveys (CE).

SOURCE OF DATA

Data for the empirical analyses of chapters 5 through 8 are from the Consumer Expenditure Survey (CE) Interviews conducted by the Bureau of Labor Statistics (BLS). The CE interview, initiated by the BLS in 1934–1936, was conducted decennially through the 1972–1973 survey. CE data are collected from a national probability sample of households designed to represent the total civilian noninstitutional population (Garner 1988). In the 1972–1973 survey, 20,000 households were interviewed on a quarterly recall basis, with the same households remaining in the sample for four quarters, so data for a full year were derived for each household.

Since 1980, the survey has been conducted on a continuous rotating panel basis, with 5,000 households interviewed quarterly for five consecutive interviews, with each quarter treated as an independent sample (Gieseman 1987). Within the sample, 20 percent of the respondents are replaced with new households each quarter. This generates a continuous design of the current data base. Data collected in the CE survey represent approximately 95 percent of all household expenditures (Gieseman 1987). The survey contains detailed information on expenditures, income, assets, and liabilities of households, as well as an array of socioeconomic and demographic characteristics.

Data files drawn from the CE samples include married-couple families under the age of sixty-five, and only nuclear families in which no other persons lived with the family. Our data files include only complete income reporters.[1] In these samples, the husband worked full-time and the wife worked either full-time or part-time or did not work.

OVERVIEW OF BOOK

The focus of this book is a comparison of the economics of dual-earner families with those of one-earner families. Chapter 2 presents economic theories and the social and economic causes of women's and wives' labor force participation. The impacts of the macroeconomic factors of inflation and wage stagnation on family income emphasize the relationships between dual-earner families and the changing U.S. economy. In Chapter 3, historical employment patterns are presented as background for discussion of the growth and development of dual-earner families. We compare the characteristics of dual- and one-earner families by socioeconomic and demographic characteristics.

In chapters 4 and 5, we present analyses and alternative scenarios of the tax treatment and employment decision making of married-couple families. The structure of federal taxes influences wives' contribution to household disposable income, and therefore to living standards. Chapter 4 is a historical overview of the major income tax policies and changes that have differently affected dual-earner and one-earner families. Costs of working generate major barriers to having two earners in the family. In Chapter 5 work-related expenditures and opportunity costs of employment of dual-earner families are discussed, with tax data and average child care costs used to calculate wives' net monetary contribution to the household.

Chapters 6 through 8 examine the comparative economic statuses of one-earner and dual-earner families, presenting the results of our empirical studies. In particular, analyses of full-time and part-time employed wives provide insights on the economic differentials between families. In these chapters, we employ several different methodologies, including descriptive and analytic statistics. Discussions of the econometric methodologies are in the chapter appendixes.

Analyses of the impact of wives' changing work roles on family expenditure patterns are presented in Chapter 6. We compare wife's work-related costs for married-couple one- and two-earner families, matched by family composition and income level. We further explore real standards of living, with analyses of expenditures of one-earner families compared with dual-earners in which the wife works full-time or part-time.

Higher-income dual-earner families might be expected to have higher savings and greater asset accumulation than one-earner families. Chapter 7 presents this issue with analysis of pre-tax and after-tax income and four types of asset data for families with the three types of wife's work status. The growth of dual-earner families has also changed the income distribution and degree of equality or inequality among different types of families.

Chapter 8 contains an analysis of the impact of wives' earnings on income distribution and inequality. We present analyses of the distribution of pre-tax and after-tax income and earnings for the three types of married-couple families.

In Chapter 9 we present our conclusions and projections for families and society. We explore the implications of the shift toward dual-earner families in terms of their lifestyles and enhanced economic security. While public policies, particularly tax policies, have significant effects on the economics of dual-earner families, causality also runs in the opposite direction. The growth of dual-earner families should be a determining factor in future policy-making.

The major objective of this book is the identification of trends and delineation of significant changes in the economic status of families. The analyses, particularly the comparative analyses of different types of families, provide much-needed input to policies that will affect the future of American families.

NOTE

1. The BLS defines complete income reporters as follows: "In general, a consumer unit who provided values for at least one of the major sources of its income, such as wages and salaries, self-employment income, and Social Security income. Even complete income reporters may not have provided a full accounting of all income from all sources" (U.S. Department of Labor 1987; Jacobs et al. 1988).

2

Economic Change and Dual-Earner Families

The importance of women's employment to the economy and to family income has undergone significant change. Increase in women's labor force participation has been particularly notable among wives, generating significant growth in the number and share of dual-income families. By the late 1970s the typical husband-wife family in the United States had two wage earners. In 1980, just over half of married women were in the labor force, making the dual-earner family more prevalent than the husband-as-sole-earner family. By 1990, the percentage had increased to 60 percent (U.S. Bureau of the Census 1990).

Wives' increased employment affected the underlying fabric of families and society. At the microeconomic level, the growth of wives' employment generated more need for child care services, wider availability of household credit, and broader affordability of housing. It also promoted household technology and influenced shopping habits and household time allocation. At the macroeconomic level, this major social change influenced the distribution of income and wealth and income tax revisions. Such changes affected consumption patterns, living standards, and markets for goods and services, and also restructured the conditions for economic and other policy-making. Increased employment of wives has generated pressures for change in both private and public institutions that remain largely predicated on the concept of a society dominated by one-earner families (Smith 1979).

The objective of this chapter is to examine increased employment of women and wives in the light of economic theory and the changing economic context of society. The next section reviews the basic economic theories that apply to the growth of women's labor force participation. An analysis of the socioeconomic reasons for women's changing economic role in the latter twentieth century follows. Next, we analyze the relationship between changing families and the changing economy by focusing on the period 1973–1986, which witnessed rising housing prices and general wage stagflation.

ECONOMIC THEORY OF WIVES' EMPLOYMENT

Economic theory, in the neoclassical tradition, emphasizes the decision making of the theoretical construct of economic man, who is viewed as acting independently to make the decisions that maximize his individual well-being. This approach, highlighting economics as a behavioral science based on the individual rather than the household unit, does not allow for the analytical conception of joint decision making within the family. The field of family economics early recognized the role of the household as the consumption unit; but only since the 1960s has mainstream economic theory expanded to consider interactive decision making within the household to maximize total family welfare (Blau and Ferber 1986). In particular, the theory has been expanded with regard to women's and wives' labor force participation decisions. This extension recognized that, in addition to paid labor force employment, unpaid in-home work provides economic value and expands consumption possibilities for the household.

Several strands of economic theory contribute to the understanding of wives' decision to work outside the home. Mincer (1962), Becker (1965), Duesenberry (1949), Strober (1977), Friedman (1955), and others developed theories about the labor force participation rates of women and specifically of married women.

Expanding upon the leisure/employment dichotomy in labor theory, Mincer (1962) introduced the concept that, particularly for married women, it is insufficient to recognize only a dichotomous work/leisure trade-off. He theorized that the demands for work at home and leisure must be taken into account in wives' labor force decisions. Further, the distribution of market employment, work at home, and leisure for each family member and among family members is determined by their relative market prices, as well as by cultural and personal factors. Mincer's analysis instigated recognition of the trade-off in the leisure/household production/employment trichotomy found in the family context of the working wife. His theory has become widely accepted in the analysis of married women's labor force behavior.

Using Mincer's concepts, Becker (1965) expanded the theory of time allocation among different pursuits, incorporating the assumption that families function as producing as well as consuming units. The strategic concept of internal input substitution within the household as an important factor in women's decision to work derives from his analysis. Becker theorized that working wives place a higher marginal value on their time available for household work than do nonemployed wives, and families with working wives therefore use more purchased goods in their household production function. This leads to the conclusion that they also spend more on labor-saving durables and appliances.

Duesenberry (1949) had earlier formulated the relative income theory, which provided an alternative view of household work and consumption decisions. He emphasized consumer decision making on the basis not only of current income but also on the household's historical income level and its position relative to other households. When income declines, the household lags in its downward adjustment, but an income increase raises the current consumption level; thus there is an asymmetry in attempts to smooth the consumption function (Dornbusch and Fischer 1981). The second hypothesis of the relative income theory is that the household is more concerned with its consumption level vis-à-vis the rest of the population than with the absolute level. Thus, utility increases only if household consumption rises relative to the average. Brady introduced a related concept of relative income. Emphasizing the neighborhood effect of the local environment on the household, she concluded that family consumption and savings depend upon the relationship between household income and average income in the area of residence. She also found saving to be negatively correlated with community income (Gilboy 1968).

Duesenberry's relative income hypothesis led Strober (1977) and others to theorize that wives work to meet peer group income and consumption levels. Strober suggested that a wife's decision to work is motivated by an income-consumption gap perceived between her own household and her reference group. She postulated that for most wives, the economic motivation to work is closely associated with the husband's earned income and the household consumption level of the family's perceived life-cycle economic and social group.

Friedman's (1955) permanent income hypothesis also contributed to the development of an economic theory of wives' employment. This theory emphasizes the long-run potential income of the household and highlights household expectations of future income rather than just current income. Friedman suggested that household income includes both permanent and transitory components, with the latter being unpredictable. The relevance of this concept to a wife's decision to work outside the home concerns the family perception of her income. The issue is whether her income is considered permanent or transitory. We find some empirical evidence that family evaluation of wife's income as permanent or transitory depends on whether she works full-time or part-time (Chapter 7). This conclusion reflects household perceptions that part-time income is transitory rather than permanent.

GROWTH IN EMPLOYMENT OF WOMEN AND WIVES

Numerous major economic and socioeconomic developments of the twentieth century have promoted women's labor force participation. These complex factors involved basic changes in society, in the roles of individuals both inside and outside the home, in the economy, and in the labor force. While many of these changes were unrelated, the concurrence of broad societal and economic changes has magnified their influence. The cumulative impact has been a fundamental revolution in women's labor force participation and, most notably, in wives' employment. In the following, we highlight several of these major trends and their economic and social effects.

Economic Change

The twentieth century has witnessed an almost complete transformation of the economic production of goods and services, particularly in the developed countries. This transformation has involved the shift from a primarily agrarian, small enterprise, home-based production economy to a major high-tech, site-based industrial economy. When most of the population worked in agriculture, the two-worker family was the norm.

Prior to the Industrial Revolution, husbands and wives contributed to the economy; both participated in the family's home-based agriculture or small business. Both provided labor input to the household production function, which included joint production for internal family consumption and for a larger external market. When economic production moved out of the individual home unit into the factory, the concept of employment changed. The family production function was transformed into one in which the husband primarily worked outside the home and the wife produced the goods and services for household consumption. As industrialization progressed and household incomes rose, increasing amounts of household goods were produced in the growing factories and purchased for household consumption. This further transformed women's in-home production role to one of providing mainly household services.

Massive industrialization and the pervasive introduction of assembly line production following World War I greatly expanded the potential for production and economic growth. This set the economic stage for post–World War II mass production, which generated an extended period of nominal and real household income growth. The mid-twentieth-century shift to a combination industrial and service-oriented economy has expanded to encompass an information-based economy. Each of these continuing economic transitions affected the role of women in society and wives' joint contributions to the family and the economy.

These broad economic transformations influenced family employment decisions, especially women's and wives' decisions to participate in the labor force. The share of families with men as the only earner peaked about 1940 (Cutler 1989). Women entered the work force in large numbers in the early 1940s, during World War II, to replace the male workers who were no longer available. However, the data do not support the long-held perception that these women remained in the labor force after the conclusion of the war, as discussed in Chapter 3. We found that following the war, many of these working women left the labor force to become full-time homemakers, as also reported by Kossoudji and Dresser (1992). Wives, in particular, left the labor force, but in a few years they started reentering. By 1948, wives were in the labor force at the same level as in 1944 (Hayghe 1990). Many in this cohort of women entered the labor force only after their families were formed and reached older ages.

As basic structural economic changes occurred, employment shares declined in agriculture and heavy manufacturing industry, and increased in services. This shift increased the demand for labor in those occupations traditionally labeled female and expanded job opportunities for women. Concurrently, the male occupational structure was changing in the 1950–1970 period, as sectoral shifts, driven by both corporate and government influences, transformed an increasing proportion of male jobs into managerial and professional categories. This change in male employment increased introductory opportunities, such as clerical labor, for women workers, further stimulating female employment. As a result of these forces, service, teaching, clerical, and medical jobs accounted for almost three-fourths of all female employment by the early 1970s (Oppenheimer 1970; Quinlan and Shackelford 1980). This changing job structure was a primary determinant of the return to dual-earner families as the norm, a situation not seen since the agrarian economy of an earlier era.

As the demand for workers in the growing service and support sectors increased, market forces changed prices and wages in these areas. Consequently, the opportunity cost of homemaking increased over time in terms of wages and other benefits forgone. This encouraged women to substitute paid labor force activity for unpaid household production (Mincer 1962; England and Farkas 1986; Blau and Winkler 1989).

Traditionally the demand for female employment was met by single women and sometimes by married women with no children or with grown children. The major sectoral changes outlined above generated a greater demand for labor than could be filled from these sources. Detailed labor market research has revealed that the postwar increase in women's labor force participation resulted primarily from employment of married women. Their labor force attachment became a distinct new trend that has persisted (Oppenheimer 1970; Smith 1979).

In analyzing trends in women's employment, Blau and Ferber (1986) distinguish between factors influencing the value of market time and those influencing the value of nonmarket time. The value of a woman's market participation is largely determined by her education, the demand for her labor, and both general and industry-specific productivity increases. Those factors influencing the value of nonmarket time include the availability of market substitutes, the degree of urbanization, demographic changes, fertility rates, level of husband's income, and family tastes and preferences.

A contrasting view of women's motivation to work outside the home was expressed by Brown (1987), who emphasized the role of social norms rather than purely economic considerations.

Since a family's housework time and money needs are determined primarily by social norms, and possibilities of substitution between time and money in maintaining the family's prescribed standard of living are limited, a wife's work decisions are not based on efficiency principles. Rather, such decisions are governed by social norms within a historical process. (Brown 1987:15)

This approach can be related to the relative income theory and its expansion to the emphasis on peer group consumption. All of the economic factors that caused women's and wives' labor force participation to expand were intensified by concurrent social trends, which further motivated female employment decisions.

Social Change

Although economic growth and technological change served as cata-
lysts drawing women into the labor force, the picture is incomplete without
acknowledgment of the interdependence between these economic changes
and dominant social trends. Changes in underlying socioeconomic and
demographic factors affected women's and wives' entry into the labor
force and their continued work attachment. The most basic of these trends
were later age at marriage and declining family size; rise in divorce rates;
increased life expectancy; higher educational levels of women; increased
social acceptance of women's employment, engendered by the civil rights
and feminist movements; and changes in household tastes for market
versus nonmarket goods and services.

With the shift from an agrarian, home-based economy to an economy
in which external market forces predominate, large families were no longer
necessary to provide the work base of the agricultural household. The high
birthrates of the beginning of the century were no longer economically
desirable. By the Great Depression of the 1930s, small families had
become the general norm, with the exception of an upward blip in the
number of children right after World War II. Average family size declined
from 3.67 in 1960 to 3.16 in 1990, while average household size fell from
3.33 to 2.62. The decline in family size was related to women's increased
median age at first marriage, from 20.3 years in 1960 to 23 in 1990 (U.S.
Bureau of the Census 1990). Interacting with tendencies toward later age
at first marriage and social preference for smaller family size, the introduction and widespread availability of contraceptives gave women expanded choice about the size of their family.

The end of World War II resulted in immediate family formations,
initiating the baby boom of 1946–1964. This baby boom, coupled with
pent-up consumer demand for housing and household products, greatly
affected the economy and family preferences. Numerous women chose to
be homemakers through the 1950s and 1960s, but as these families
matured and child-rearing functions ended, many decided to enter the
labor force.

Other demographic factors, including higher levels of education, encouraged the emerging trend toward increased female employment.
Women found a two-way relationship between their education levels and
job participation. As they obtained more and higher education, their
employment skills and marketability expanded, and their potential earnings increased. Simultaneously, expanded demand for women workers

served as an inducement to their further education and training for better-paying jobs.

As these sociodemographic changes occurred, the civil rights and feminist movements furthered social acceptance of women's work. The Civil Rights Act of 1964, which legalized the concept of equal pay for equal work, had a major influence on both attitudes toward and opportunities for employed women. Overall, its societal impact was even greater for women's economic role and labor force participation than for those of minorities.

The feminist movement also affected attitudes and social norms regarding women's work. As women expanded their work efforts outside the home, more and more social and economic responses supported this major transition: child care facilities expanded, stores increased their open hours, the fashion industry responded with work-oriented styles, and the food industry promoted prepared meals and fast foods. Within the family, tastes and preferences for market over nonmarket goods and services evolved in conjunction with women's and wives' employment. When working women and dual-earner families became more the norm, spousal attitudes began to adapt to the new reality, especially among younger families.

Another issue concerns the stage at which women commit to the labor force. The usual assumption that women make the decision to work after marriage may have been the case through the prefeminist era, but this can no longer be assumed. Today, many women have committed to the labor force prior to marriage, so the issue of employment becomes a part of the marital decision for both partners. Thus, two-earner families are often initiated at marriage rather than after marriage by the wife's subsequent entry into the labor force. Dual-earner families are formed by women and men who began their careers with equal training, education, and career commitment. The fact that there will be two earners is taken for granted in these married-couple families.

ECONOMIC TRANSITION AND WORKING WOMEN

Following over a quarter-century of unprecedented economic growth, three important and interrelated economic trends occurred during the period 1973–1986: the continuing rise in women's labor force participation, the general stagnation of wages in the United States, and generally rising prices (Danziger 1980; Betson and van der Gaag 1984; Minarik 1988). This proved to be a period of transition for families, faced with the shift from an extended period of rapid economic expansion to one of slower growth, high inflation, and sometimes stagflation. In sum, a changing economy confronted changing households. In particular, families faced rising prices for housing during a time when real earnings, especially for men, tended to stagnate.

Housing Inflation

Since 1970, substantial inflation in housing prices and the increased perception of housing as a capital investment have motivated women's employment. As housing prices rose, families sought to purchase newer and larger homes, which required higher total household income to finance and to make large monthly payments. The Equal Credit Opportunity Act of 1975 allowed the use of wives' earnings as part of household income to qualify for mortgages. As households locked into larger mortgage payments, wives' employment became more of a necessity. In addition, it became important as a hedge against husbands' possible unemployment. Having two regular earners proved to be the most important form of family unemployment insurance.

Wage Stagflation

Following an extended expansionary period, there was a notable decline in the growth of real household income from 1973 through the 1980s. Real wages stagnated, and if the two-earner family had not become increasingly prevalent, average household income (adjusted for inflation) would have grown even less than actually occurred (Levy 1988a; Litan et al. 1988). After rising for nearly three decades, men's real earnings were virtually flat during the 1970s. A paradox of this period was that while earnings per worker stagnated, income per capita increased from $9,926 (in 1987 dollars) to $12,150 in 1987. This apparent contradiction was caused primarily by increased women's labor force participation and two-paycheck families, and secondarily by the smaller families related to wives' employment (Levy 1988b).

Many women entered the labor market or increased their participation to improve or maintain their household standard of living (Blank 1988). Families with full-time working wives increased their share of both income and assets, in contrast to other household types (Rubin and Riney 1989). These trends verify the thesis expounded by Duesenberry, and later applied by Strober, that women become employed to raise their household living standards to that of a perceived peer group.

SUMMARY AND CONCLUSIONS

Advances in economic theory have contributed to our ability to explain wives' increased labor force participation. In particular, expansion of the leisure/work dichotomy to a trichotomy that includes placing a value on in-home production and the strategic concept of internal input substitution within the household clarifies wives' employment decision making. Application of the theories of relative income and of permanent versus transitory income enable evaluation of wives' monetary contribution to total household income and consumption possibilities.

Broad changes in the economy and in society established the conditions that promoted women's movement into the labor force in large numbers. The change from an agrarian to an industrial economy with mass production, necessitated by World War II, brought married women into the labor force in greater numbers. The shift to a predominantly service-sector economy provided greater employment opportunities for female workers, increasing their opportunity cost of not working. These economic factors were intensified by changes in major social trends that encouraged women's and wives' employment. Later age at marriage and smaller family size meant that increasing numbers of women spent more time in the labor force. As job opportunities grew, women obtained higher levels of education and social acceptance of women's employment expanded.

The period from the early 1970s through the 1980s was of particular importance in the expansion of wives' labor force participation. Rising prices combined with wage stagnation for male workers generated a period of transition for families. Many wives worked to implement desired lifestyles and to finance higher housing costs.

Most of these broad economic and social trends appear to be slowing or stabilizing as families move into the next century. Over 60 percent of married women under age sixty-five are now working, and the share of nonemployed wives is projected to continue declining (Waldrop 1989). The expansion of household consumption has slowed, inflation has not been excessive in recent years, and the extended spiral in the price of housing has slowed or ceased. Consequently, we conclude that the predictions of the relative income hypothesis will be less applicable in the future, since wives' income is widely perceived as permanent rather than transitory. Household lifestyle will depend upon dual-earner families and working wives will be the expectation.

3

Labor Force Participation and Characteristics of Married-Couple Families

The married-couple family continues to be a dominant social and economic institution in America despite the profound changes it has undergone. In 1920 almost 85 percent of households were married couples (Hayghe 1990), compared with 75 percent by 1960. After years of decline, this share plateaued during the 1980s to about 60 percent by 1990 (U.S. Bureau of the Census 1991). Although their share of households has declined, married-couple families contain 70 percent of all Americans because they are larger on average than other households (U.S. Bureau of the Census 1991).

As households have become more diverse, the labor force participation of family members has undergone significant change. Married women enter and remain in the labor force in increasing numbers. The married couple with a working husband and homemaker wife is a declining minority. Only 17 percent of married-couple families fit this description in 1992, compared with 35 percent in 1967 (Figure 3.1). While the share of married-couple families with the husband as the only earner halved, the share with the wife as the only earner doubled, but is still only 4 percent. In 1992 both the husband and wife were employed in 60 percent of married-couple families, up from 43 percent in 1967.

Dual-earner families are a vital segment of the population with crucial economic impacts that are even greater than their numbers would indicate. Dual-earner couples provide insulation against the insecurity of economic cycles or the unemployment of one family member. Overall, they are among the higher-income households, home owners, and spenders.

Figure 3.1
The Changing Labor Force Patterns of Married-Couple Families,
1967–1992

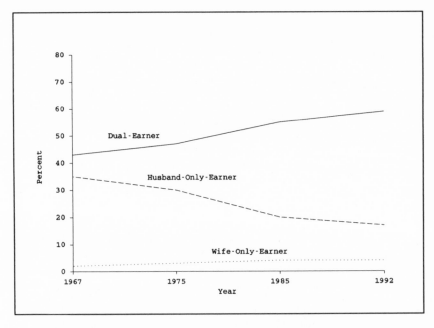

Sources: U.S. Department of Labor, Bureau of Labor Statistics (1989b). *Handbook of Labor Statistics*. Bulletin 2340 (August), pp. 235–256. U.S. Department of Labor, Bureau of Labor Statistics (1992). *Marital and Family Characteristics of the Labor Force from the March 1992 Current Population Survey* Unpublished data.

This chapter presents a compilation of information that is unique because there is a paucity of published data on married-couple families or on husbands and wives as earners. Detailed data are available on men and women in the labor force, but less so for husbands and wives or married couples. The Bureau of Labor Statistics annually collects and publishes data on the labor force by types of households, marital status of workers, and selected demographic characteristics.

The first part of this chapter presents the labor force participation of men and women, of husbands and wives, and of married-couple families. We survey the historical context of changes in labor force participation, with emphasis on the number and share of employed wives in dual-earner families. The second part describes the composition and demographic characteristics of dual-earner families. This is followed by an analysis of the impact of demographic changes on married-couple family incomes,

Figure 3.2
Labor Force Participation Rates[a] (%) of Men, Women, Husbands, and Wives,[b] 1890–1991

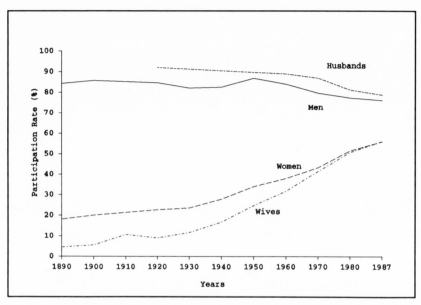

[a]Prior to 1947, data based on population age 14 and over; thereafter 16 years and over.
[b]Includes a small share with husband absent.

Sources: U.S. Department of Commerce, Bureau of the Census, 1890–1970 Historical Statistics of the United States Colonial Times to 1970, Bicentennial Edition, Part 1. U.S. Bureau of the Census, Statistical Abstract of the United States: 1992 (112th edition) Washington DC, 1991. U.S. Department of Labor, Bureau of Labor Statistics, Handbook of Labor Statistics, Bulletin 2340, August 1989.

earnings, and living standards. In some cases we compare one-earner and dual-earner families with all married-couple families, which includes retired, unemployed, and some other family types.

LABOR FORCE PARTICIPATION

Labor force participation is presented as the rates of labor force participation of specific groups—men, women, husbands, wives—and by disaggregated demographic groups such as age and income. These rates are calculated as the percentage of a population group that is employed and/or looking for work. For example, the 1990 labor force rate of participation for wives, 58.5 percent, represents the number of wives employed and/or

Table 3.1
Labor Force Participation Rates[a] (%) of Men, Women, Husbands, and Wives, 1890–1991

Year	Men	Women	Husbands	Wives[b]
1890	84.3	18.2	n.a.	4.6
1900	85.7	20.0	n.a.	5.6
1910	n.a.	n.a.	n.a.	10.7
1920	84.6	22.7	92.0	9.0
1930	82.1	23.6	n.a.	11.7
1940	82.5	27.9	n.a.	16.7
1950	86.8	33.9	n.a.	24.8
1960	84.0	37.8	88.9	31.7
1970	79.7	43.3	86.9	41.4
1980	77.4	51.5	81.2	50.7
1987	76.2	56.0	78.8	56.1
1991	75.5	57.3	78.0	58.6

[a]Prior to 1947, data based on population age 14 and over; thereafter 16 years and over.
[b]Includes a small share with husband absent.

Sources: U.S. Department of Commerce, Bureau of the Census (1975). 1890–1970 Historical Statistics of the United States Colonial Times to 1970, Bicentennial Edition, Part 1. U.S. Bureau of the Census, Statistical Abstract of the United States: 1992 (112th edition) Washington DC, 1991. U.S. Department of Labor, Bureau of Labor Statistics, Handbook of Labor Statistics, Bulletin 2340, August 1989.

actively looking for work (31 million) divided by the number of all wives (53 million).

Men

The strikingly different long-term trends of men's and women's employment status are presented in Table 3.1. Since 1890, the male labor force participation rate averaged a fairly steady 85 percent. Male employment peaked after World War II, as servicemen returned to the civilian labor force, followed by a steady long-term decline beginning in the 1960s. The significant shift in male participation rates, from 87 to 75 percent, has been in the opposite direction from female participation rates. In the 1960s, when women and wives entered the labor force in increasing numbers, men were leaving or retiring earlier.

Several social and economic factors influenced the decreasing male participation rate. Age at retirement has declined substantially, resulting in a significant decrease in the numbers of older workers (age fifty-five and over) (Hayghe and Haugen 1987). Coincident to earlier retirement, life expectancy has increased. More men are living to age sixty-five, reducing the share of all men who are employed.

Many men have retired earlier as both policy and household economic changes have increased household economic security. The introduction and growth of Social Security and disability benefits, as well as the expansion and strengthening of pensions, promoted earlier retirement. The indexing of Social Security and some indemnity pensions enhanced the real value of retirement income. Concurrently, wives' employment increased the economic security of many families, which may increase total household income from Social Security and a second pension.

Women

From the beginning of the twentieth century to 1991, the male participation rate declined 12 percent while the female participation rate increased by 185 percent. The share of women workers increased from 20 to 57 percent and the share of married women increased from 6 to 59 percent (Table 3.1). In 1991, three-quarters of the 56 million women in the labor force worked full-time (35 hours or more per week). Almost 60 percent of the full-timers worked the entire year, while only 10 percent of the part-time women worked full-year (U.S. Department of Labor 1991).

Shifts in several major sociodemographic factors contributed to the significant growth in women's labor force participation. The rise in the divorce rate between 1960 and 1980 accounts for 17 percent of women's increased participation during that period (Lichter and Costanzo 1987). Three-fourths of divorced women are in the labor force (U.S. Department of Labor 1991). Further, women's median age at first marriage has increased by more than three and a half years since 1960, leaving more young single women as labor market participants (U.S. Department of Commerce, Bureau of the Census 1990b). Single women have traditionally maintained relatively high rates of labor force participation, with 80 percent employed since the 1960s (Shank 1988). Another notable aspect of women's increased work rates is the growth in labor force participation of older women. The proportion of working women over age fifty-five has doubled since 1950 to more than 40 percent (Herz 1988). However, the most significant factor contributing to the growth of women's employment in recent decades is the increased participation of married women with young children. Their employment grew to 60 percent (U.S. Department of Labor 1991).

Women's educational upgrading has served as an additional motivator of their employment. Median years of schooling and the share of women completing high school have substantially increased. Greater educational attainment alters the relative importance of the choice between work at home and labor market participation. The opportunity cost of not working, in terms of higher forgone wages and salaries, increases with the level of education. This factor has been particularly notable for the cohort of women who are baby boomers. This cohort, born in the 1950s and entering the labor force in the 1970s, shifted the age distribution of the female labor force. The maturing of the baby-boom cohort increased the number of women in the age categories most likely to be in the labor force. Overall, these continuing patterns of demographic change account for almost half of the increase in female labor force participation (Lichter and Costanzo 1987).

Husbands

The historical labor force trends for husbands and wives followed the same broad patterns as for all men and women but were even more dramatic (Table 3.1). Husbands consistently have had a higher labor force attachment, higher earnings, and lower unemployment than all males. Since 60 percent of males are married, husbands' strong labor force attachment is a major factor in males' high participation rates. Historical data on husbands in the labor force were not collected prior to 1960. In fact, research on husbands' employment has lagged because it has been overshadowed by the much larger labor force changes of wives (Hayghe and Haugen 1987). Since 1920, husbands' participation rate has decreased from 92 to 78 percent (Hayghe 1990).

Several factors—including educational level, work experience, occupational category, and motivation to earn—influence husbands' high participation rates. Husbands are more educated than other men, their work experience is more continuous and consistent, and they are more heavily concentrated in white-collar occupations (Hayghe and Haugen 1987).

Wives

Given societal attitudes and the lack of household technology, it was not surprising to find that in a 1920 study wives indicated the reasons they worked outside the home were the need to support large families, inadequacy of husband's wages, inflation, providing for their children's education, and saving for old age. In a subsequent survey during the 1920s, 80 percent of wives who were job applicants indicated that economic necessity was the reason they were seeking employment (Hayghe 1990). The

Table 3.2
Number and Percent of Wives in the Labor Force, 1890–1991

Year	Number in Labor Force (000s)	Employed Wives As Percent (%) Of		
		Total Labor Force	Women in Labor Force	All Wives
1890	515	2.2	13.9	4.6
1900	769	2.7	15.4	5.6
1910[a]	1,891	5.1	24.7	10.7
1920	1,920	4.7	23.0	9.0
1930	3,071	6.3	28.9	11.7
1940	5,040	9.5	36.4	16.7
1950	9,273	14.6	52.1	24.8
1960	13,485	19.4	59.9	31.7
1970	19,799	23.9	63.4	41.4
1980	26,828	25.1	59.7	50.7
1987	31,282	26.1	59.1	56.1
1991	33,318	26.9	59.1	58.6

Note: Prior to 1947, based on population age 14 and over; thereafter 16 years and over. "Wives" includes a small share with husband absent.

[a]1910 data aberrant because it includes women not enumerated in other years.

Sources: U.S. Department of Commerce, Bureau of the Census (1975). 1890–1970 Historical statistics of the United States Colonial Times to 1970, Bicentennial Edition, Part 1. U.S. Bureau of the Census, Statistical Abstract of the United States: Washington DC, 1950. U.S. Department of Labor, Bureau of Labor Statistics, Marital and Family Characteristics of the Labor Force from March 1991 Current Population Survey, September.

situation for working wives has changed in many respects, but many still perceive their contribution to household income as the driving force in their decision to enter or remain in the labor force.

In striking contrast to husbands, wives had much lower labor force participation rates than all women until 1960, when the gap began to close swiftly. Less than 6 percent of wives worked outside the home at the turn of the century, and it took thirty years for this very low share to double (Table 3.1). By 1950 one-fourth of wives were employed, but this was only three-quarters as many wives as all women. In the ensuing decades, this gap decreased. By 1991, 59 percent of wives (33 million) were in the labor force, more than twice the 1950 rate. This surpassed the proportion (57 percent) of all women in the labor force.

The spectacular changes that have occurred in wives' labor force participation warrant a more detailed analysis. Table 3.2 presents the number of wives in the labor force for selected years since 1890 and historical data calculated for employed wives as a percent of the total labor force and of women workers, as well as of all wives. In this historical data, "wives" includes a small share with husband absent.

The share of working wives as a percent of the total labor force (Table 3.2, column 3) steadily increased from 2 percent in 1890 to 27 percent in 1991. Over this period, the highest rates of growth occurred during the 1930s and 1940s. In the 1930s the rate of growth was over 50 percent. This was a response to declines in household incomes or in share of male workers due to the Great Depression. The largest rate of increase (54 percent) occurred during the 1940s, when married women entered the labor force in large numbers to replace men serving in the military. During the 1950s and 1960s, the rate of growth started declining, and since 1970 it has been less than 1 percent.

During the twentieth century, the share of employed wives as a percent of women workers (Table 3.2, column 4) grew from 15 to 59 percent, a fourfold increase. However, this share peaked in 1970 at 63 percent and has since dropped to virtually the same level as in 1960. The most dramatic change occurred in the share of wives in the labor force, from 6 to 59 percent, shown in column 5 of Table 3.2. Thus, wives' labor force participation rate and working wives as a share both of women workers and of all wives are now very close. Approximately six out of ten wives in any of these categories are employed.

The greatest rate of increase (43 percent) in the share of wives working occurred during the 1930s. Recognition of this change in wives' labor force participation during the decade of the Great Depression has not previously been noted in the literature. Following 1940, the rate of increase in the share of wives employed continued to increase at a slower rate until 1970, after which it declined. The share of wives working may have approached a saturation point, and future increases are likely to be marginally smaller than in the past.

There are increasing numbers of married-couple families in which the wife is the sole earner. In 1970, fewer than one million of all married-couple families had the wife as the only earner, but by 1992 both the number and share had doubled.

Wives' labor force participation rates have increased dramatically for every age group under sixty-five, with the greatest increases for those between ages twenty and forty-five (Table 3.3). From 1960 to 1980, the participation rates for wives aged twenty to thirty-five doubled, and have continued to increase. Wives aged thirty-five to forty-five also now participate at more than twice their rates for 1960.

Table 3.3

Labor Force Participation Rates (%) of Wives by Age, 1960–1991

Year	16-19	20-24	25-34	35-44	45-64	65+
1960	25.3	30.0	27.7	36.2	34.2	5.9
1970	36.0	47.4	39.3	47.2	44.1	7.9
1980	47.7	60.5	59.3	62.5	46.9	7.2
1990	50.0	66.5	69.8	74.0	56.5	8.5
1991	48.7	65.0	70.1	74.3	57.1	8.3

Source: U.S. Bureau of the Census (1992). Statistical Abstract of the United States: 1992 (112th ed.). Washington, DC.

While the labor force participation rate for wives increased by 84 percent between 1960 and 1991 (Table 3.4, column 2), the share of wives working full-time (22 million) versus part-time (8 million) has remained relatively stable. The share of those working full-time declined slightly during the 1960s but since that time has remained quite stable at almost three-fourths, the same as that for all employed women. Many wives who work part-time have chosen this alternative in order to care for children or elders, or to fulfill other responsibilities. The proportion working part-time involuntarily is closely related to trends in the macroeconomy, rising during recessions. About one of seven part-time working wives would have preferred full-time employment (U.S. Department of Labor 1989a). The employment status of those who work part-time, but not by choice, has real disadvantages. Earnings are less, even after allowing for their lesser costs incurred by working, and fringe benefits are usually not available or at best limited.

Wives with Children

Increasing numbers of married women with spouse present entered and remained in the labor force, regardless of the presence and age of their children. This is in significant contrast to the situation as late as 1977, when the Bureau of the Census reported, "The age of the child is often a critical factor in determining whether the mother enters or remains in the labor force. The participation rate for wives whose only children at home were age 14 to 17 was about 57 percent, while the rate for those whose children were all under 6 was only 40 percent" (U.S. Department of Commerce, Bureau of the Census 1977). Table 3.4 reveals the widely noted trend of increased labor force participation for wives both with and

Table 3.4
Labor Force Participation Rates (%) of Wives[a] by Presence and Age of Children, 1960–1991

			With Children				
Year	All Wives	No Child < 18	< 18	6-17	< 6	3-5	< 3
1960	32	35	28	39	19	n.a.	n.a.
1970	41	42	40	49	30	n.a.	n.a.
1980	51	46	54	62	45	52	41
1987	56	48	64	71	57	61	54
1991	59	51	67	74	60	65	67
Share Employed Full-Time[b]:							
1960	77	82	71	72	70	n.a.	n.a.
1970	73	79	67	68	65	n.a.	n.a.
1980	72	77	67	69	65	67	64
1987	73	78	68	71	64	66	63
1991	74	78	70	72	68	68	67
Share Employed Part-Time[c]:							
1960	23	18	29	28	30	n.a.	n.a.
1970	27	21	33	32	35	n.a.	n.a.
1980	28	23	33	31	35	33	37
1987	27	22	32	29	36	34	37
1991	26	22	30	28	32	32	33

[a]Married women, spouse present.
[b]Persons who usually worked 35 hours or more per week.
[c]Persons who usually worked less than 35 hours per week.

Sources: 1960–1987 data: U.S. Dept. of Labor Bureau of Labor Statistics (1989b). Handbook of Labor Statistics Bulletin 2340 (August). 1991 data: U.S. Dept. of Labor Bureau of Labor Statistics (1991). Marital and Family Characteristics of the Labor Force from the March 1991 Current Population Survey, Unpublished data: Full-time and part-time were calculated.

without children. Growth in the participation rates of wives with children under age eighteen has been much more rapid than for those without. One reason is that wives who have never had children tend toward earlier retirement. Another is that the increased labor force attachment of mothers is probably age-related, that is, younger wives with the strongest labor force attachment are in the life-cycle stage of establishing a family.

Among wives with children, the most notable increase in labor force participation occurred for married women with preschool children (under age six). Their employment rate more than tripled since 1960 and doubled from 30 to 60 percent between 1970 and 1991. Since 1960, participation has not quite doubled for those with school age children (from six to eighteen years), and it increased less than fifty percent for wives with no children under age eighteen.

Despite the dramatic increases in the number and proportion of employed wives, the share working full-time declined during the 1960s (Table 3.4), possibly due to general prosperity in the economy and increased incomes of husbands. For wives without children under age eighteen, the share employed full-time has remained virtually constant since 1970. For those with children at home, full-time employment participation has gradually returned to the 1960 level. Only for families with children in the school-age group (six to seventeen) did the share of wives working full-time increase.

Labor force participation of wives with younger preschool-age children presented a different picture. Larger shares worked part-time through 1987, and then a new trend developed with increases in full-time working mothers of children under age three. This reveals the strength of younger wives' labor force commitment. For those with children under six, there was increased full-time employment between 1987 and 1991 (U.S. Department of Labor, Bureau of Labor Statistics 1991; U.S. Department of Labor, Bureau of Labor Statistics 1989b.).

In sum, although many more wives work outside the home, the share of employed married women working part-time slowly but steadily increased from 1960 through the late 1980s, and then declined from 1987 to 1991. This occurred whether they had children or not. For those with children under eighteen years of age, the share working full-time declined until 1987 and then rose again. The most dramatic change in employment status occurred from 1987 to 1991 among full-time working wives with preschool children.

The share working part-time has increased almost one-fourth since 1960 for those with no children under age eighteen. This might be due to the lesser financial burden on families without children or to a desire to be in the labor force on a limited basis. Alternatively, these wives may not have been able to find desired full-time employment, as increasing numbers of employers have reduced their full-time work force to cut costs.

Dual-Earner Families

The increases in working wives have resulted in significant changes in U.S. families. Dual-earner families are more prevalent now than single-earner families and constitute three-fifths of all families. In 1920, when most households were married couples, only 9 percent were dual-earner. By the 1940s, the three million dual-earner families were

Table 3.5
Husbands and Other Family Members in the Labor Force, 1960–1988

Year	Husbands in Labor Force (000's)	Percent Distribution			
		Husband Only	Husband and Wife	Husband, Wife, and Others	Other Member Only
1960	35,041	57.0	25.8	6.2	11.1
1970	38,639	46.9	34.5	9.3	9.3
1980	39,907	35.0	44.8	12.2	8.1
1988	40,781	27.7	53.0	13.3	6.0

Note: Married, spouse present; excludes married couples living in households where a relative is the householder.

Sources: U.S. Department of Labor, Bureau of Labor Statistics (1989b). Handbook of Labor Statistics, Bulletin 2340, August.

still only 9 percent of all families. In the following decade this share surged, and then it continued to grow by an average of 700,000 a year after 1965 (Hayghe 1990). As many as two-thirds of young married couples begin marriage as dual-earners, with both partners already employed (Levy and Michel 1991). Figure 3.1 illustrates these trends in family labor force patterns.

As increasing numbers of wives have entered the labor force, there are fewer married couples with the husband as the sole earner (Table 3.5). The inverse relationship between the shares of one-earner and dual-earner families is clear. Since the 1960s, households with only the husband working have declined from 57 percent to 28 percent, while the share with working wives has increased from 26 to 53 percent. Married-couple families with both the wife and other family members working more than doubled to 13 percent.

Most husbands of working wives are employed full-time, and the share of wives working full-time continues to increase. The share of all wives who worked full-time increased from 44 to 50 percent from 1981 to 1987, while the share of wives in dual-earner families who worked full-time increased from 66 to 68 percent. In both 1981 and 1987, only 12 percent of working wives had husbands who either worked part-time or were unemployed (U.S. Department of Commerce, Bureau of the Census 1989a).

Table 3.6

Demographic Characteristics of Married-Couple Families, 1990 (number in thousands)

Characteristics	All	Dual-Earner		Husband-Only-Earner	
		Number	Percent[a]	Number	Percent[b]
Size of City					
>2.5 Mil.	15,373	8,202	38	4,255	42
1-2.5 Mil.	9,100	5,139	24	2,097	21
250,000-1 Mil.	10,093	5,484	26	2,550	25
<250,000	4,942	2,643	12	1,182	12
Size of Family					
Two	20,656	8,718	31	3,600	28
Three	11,527	6,941	25	3,006	23
Four	12,264	8,033	29	3,477	27
Five or More	7,869	4,363	16	2,808	22
Own Children by Age					
None <18	27,780	12,288	44	5,347	41
<18	24,537	15,768	56	7,667	59
<6 Only	6,473	3,805	14	2,470	19
6-17 Only	12,485	8,836	31	2,975	23
Age of Householder					
15-29	6,482	4,317	15	1,928	15
30-44	19,622	13,676	49	5,320	41
45-59	13,302	8,272	29	3,643	30
60+	12,912	1,790	6	2,122	16

[a]Percent of all dual-earner.
[b]Percent of all husband-only-earner.

Sources: U.S. Department of Commerce, Bureau of the Census (1990a). Household and Family Characteristics: March 1990 and 1989, Current Population Reports No. 447, Population Characteristics, Series P-20.

DEMOGRAPHIC CHARACTERISTICS OF DUAL-EARNER FAMILIES

As dual-earners have become the primary family form, their impacts on society and the economy have continued to grow, so it is particularly useful to examine their characteristics. The following sections describe demographic and income characteristics of dual-earner compared with one-earner married-couple families.

Location, Size of Family, and Age of Children

In Table 3.6 we compare several demographic characteristics of dual-earner families with husband-only-earner and with all married-couple families. Dual-earner families are evenly distributed in terms of their urbanization. Over half of all married couples in cities of each size category are dual-earner, with an additional 24 to 28 percent one-earner. The rest include retired couples, wife-only-earners, families with no earners, and others.

There is greater disparity when examining married-couple households by size of family. The largest share (31 percent) of dual-earner families are two-person, 25 percent are three-person, 29 percent are four-person, and 16 percent are larger than four-person. Out of all two-person married-couple families, 42 percent are dual-earner, and 17 percent are one-earner. This is partly attributable to the increasing numbers of retired or nonworking couples. Of four-person households, two-thirds are dual-earner; the largest share of one-earners is in families with five or more persons.

There are twice as many dual-earner families with children under eighteen as one-earner. Among dual-earner households, 44 percent have no children under age eighteen, compared with 41 percent for one-earner. For families with children aged six to seventeen only, three times as many are dual-earner as one-earner. Almost 60 percent of married-couple families with children less than six are dual-earner. This highlights the strong work attachment of younger married women, even when they have preschool children. Their increased work status correlates closely with their rising levels of educational attainment. "Regardless of whether a wife has children or not, the more years of school she has completed, the more likely she is to be a member of the labor force" (U.S. Department of Commerce, Bureau of the Census 1977:23).

Joint Education Level

Dual-earner families have higher levels of education than other married couples, with both husbands and wives having at least completed high school in 83 percent (Table 3.7). The 16 percent share of dual-earner families in which both spouses are college graduates is higher than for other married couples, and in an additional 20 percent either husband or wife has completed college. In half of dual-earner families, the wife has more than a high school education, compared with 41 percent for all married couples and 37 percent when the husband is the only earner.

Table 3.7

Married-Couple Families by Joint Education Level, 1988 (numbers in thousands)

Education Level (in years)	All[a]		Dual-Earner		Husband-Only-Earner	
	Number	Percent	Number	Percent	Number	Percent
Total	51,809	100	27,016	100	13,737	100
Both <12	6,433	12	1,612	6	1,793	13
Husband 12,Wife Less	2,696	5	978	4	980	7
Wife 12,Husband Less	4,286	8	1,791	7	998	7
Both Husband and Wife 12	12,407	24	6,796	25	3,392	25
Husband 13-15, Wife Less	4,486	9	2,360	9	1,331	10
Wife 13-15, Husband Less	3,205	6	1,992	7	629	5
Both 13-15	3,007	6	2,002	7	700	3
Husband 16+, Wife Less	6,349	12	3,404	13	2,045	15
Wife 16+, Husband Less	2,661	5	1,814	7	417	3
Both Husband and Wife 16+	6,280	12	4,268	16	1,451	11

aIncludes unemployed, not in labor force, retired, and wife-only-earner.

Sources: U.S. Department of Commerce, Bureau of the Census (1989b). Household and Family Characteristics: March 1988, Current Population Reports, Population Characteristics, Series P-20, No. 437.

Women who are college graduates are 24 percent more likely to be in the labor force and earn 40 percent more than those with only a high school education (Bergman 1986). Higher education expands employment opportunities both in status and in earnings. As expected, with higher levels of educational attainment, income and earnings are higher for dual-earner married couples than for families with husband as only-earner.

INCOME AND EARNINGS OF DUAL-EARNER FAMILIES

The dramatic changes in wives' employment status are reflected in the incomes and financial resources of dual-earner families relative to other households. The growth of the two-earner family emphasizes the importance of the family as the unit of analysis in income studies and indicates that family earnings may be a more appropriate index of well-being than individual measures of income (Smith 1979). In this section, we analyze

Table 3.8
**Median Money Income of Married-Couple Families in Current and
Constant 1990 Dollars, 1970–1990**

	1970	1975	1980	1985	1990
Current Dollars					
Total Married Couples	$10,516	$14,867	$23,141	$31,100	$39,895
Dual-Earner	12,276	17,237	26,879	36,431	46,777
Husband-Only-Earner	9,304	12,752	18,972	24,556	30,265
Constant 1990 Dollars					
Total Married Couples	35,424	36,117	36,705	37,777	38,547
Dual-Earner	41,352	41,875	42,635	44,252	46,777
Husband-Only-Earner	31,341	30,979	30,093	29,828	30,265

Source: U.S. Bureau of the Census (1992). Statistical Abstract of the United States: 1992
        (112th ed.). Washington, DC.

incomes of married-couple families, the effects of occupations on earnings, and family earnings. To show the special characteristics of dual-
earner families, we compare them with husband-only-earner families.

Income of Dual-Earner Families

The increase in wives' labor force participation affected household
incomes. In general, the average income of households, which includes
single persons, is greater than the average income of families, which
includes lower-income single-parent families. The 1990 median money
income of one-earner families, $30,265, was only two-thirds that of
dual-earner families, $46,777 (Table 3.8). This difference is even more
compelling when viewed over time. In 1970, husband-only-earner family
income was three-fourths that of dual-earner families, so the income gap
has widened over time. The real income or constant-dollar purchasing
power comparison is even more meaningful. In constant 1990 dollars,
one-earner real income has declined, while dual-earner family median real
income has increased by $5,425 (13 percent) since 1970. This growth in
the purchasing power of dual-earner families is attributable to both increased numbers of employed wives and their increased earnings.

Table 3.9
Married-Couple Families by Income Level, 1991 (numbers in thousands)

Income Level	All	Dual-Earner		Husband-Only-Earner	
		Number	Percent[a]	Number	Percent[a]
Families					
<$12,499	3,981	710	18	970	24
$12,500-19,999	5,246	1,533	29	1,257	24
$20,000-39,999	17,011	7,989	46	3,446	20
$40,000-59,999	12,805	7,097	55	1,819	14
>$60,000	13,198	6,654	50	1,616	12
Families with Children <18					
<$12,499	1,531	412	27	739	48
$12,500-19,999	2,063	854	41	867	42
$20,000-39,999	8,053	4,760	59	2,698	34
$40,000-59,999	6,660	4,797	72	1,668	25
>$60,000	6,130	4,670	76	1,334	22

[a]Percent of all married-couple families in that income group.

Sources: Compiled from U.S. Department of Labor, Bureau of Labor Statistics (1991). Marital and Labor Characteristics of the Labor Force from the March 1991 Current Population Survey Unpublished data (September).

Wives' work status also affects the income distribution of families, so it differs by type of married-couple family, as shown in Table 3.9. The share of all married-couple families who are dual-earner increases with income level, while the share in which the husband is the only earner decreases with income level. Only 18 percent of married-couple families with incomes under $12,500, approximately the federal poverty level for a family of four persons in 1991, are dual-earner, while almost a fourth are one-earner. The other 58 percent are either retired or unemployed. For the income level $20,000 to $40,000, 46 percent of married couples are dual-earner, compared with only 20 percent with husband as the only earner. The dual-earner share increases to 55 percent for $40,000 to $60,000, and is 50 percent for incomes over $60,000; it is 14 and 12 percent, respectively, for one-earner families.

The numbers of dual-earner and husband-only-earner families with children under age eighteen follow the same general income distribution pattern, but with considerably higher shares as income increases. Notably, about three-quarters of dual-earner married-couple families with income over $40,000 have children under eighteen, while virtually all the remainder are one-earner.

In general, the increased number of dual-earner families has had a significant effect on the distribution of family income. Dual-earner families are moving to higher quartiles of the income distribution, leaving one-earner households in the lower quartiles, particularly those that are headed by a single parent. This increases the degree of income inequality.

Earnings of Dual-Earner Families

The family incomes described include income from all sources and all household earners, while earnings include only wages and salaries. Both the husband and wife worked in almost three-fourths of the 43.5 million married couples. All married couples had median earnings of $39,208 in 1991, compared with earnings of $45,968 for dual-earner families (U.S. Bureau of the Census 1992).

Mean earnings of husbands and wives in married-couple families with different characteristics are compared in Table 3.10. Wives' 1987 average earnings were less than half those of husbands, and this relationship was similar regardless of wives' education level. However, from 1981 to 1987 wives' real earnings (in constant 1987 dollars) increased almost twice as fast as husbands'. For any of the demographic subcategories compared, wives' real earnings grew faster than husbands', except those age sixty and over.

Despite the more rapid rate of growth of wives' real earnings, the ratio of wives' to husbands' earnings remains low. When both worked full-time, wives' earnings were 54 percent of husbands'. When both worked part-time, wives' earnings were two-thirds those of husbands who had very low earnings. These ratios by work experience reflect that more wives held part-time jobs than husbands, 79 percent of whom worked year-round full-time (U.S. Bureau of the Census 1991). Only for younger workers, age thirty-five or less, were wives' earnings more than half as large as those of husbands, which might have been due to the availability of service jobs for young women.

Although the vast majority of husbands earn more than their wives, there are dual-earner families in which the wife earns more, has a more prestigious job, and has less unemployment. In 1987, there were over 5 million wives (18 percent) whose earnings were greater than their husbands'. These wives were likely to work full-time and full-year, to have completed at least some college, and to have no children at home. They also tended to be in executive, professional, or administrative support occupations (U.S. Department of Commerce, Bureau of the Census

Table 3.10

Mean Earnings in Constant 1987 Dollars of Husbands and Wives by Selected Characteristics, 1981 and 1987

Characteristics	Husband			Wife		
	1981	1987	Percent Change	1981	1987	Percent Change
Total	$26,075	$29,154	11.8	$10,744	$13,245	23.3
Age						
15-24	15,468	15,028	-2.9	8,039	8,791	9.4
25-34	23,382	25,238	7.9	11,013	13,077	18.7
35-44	30,204	33,166	9.8	11,227	14,764	31.5
45-54	29,914	34,648	15.8	11,509	14,094	22.5
55-64	27,334	28,727	5.1	11,024	12,251	11.1
65+	13,325	16,132	21.1	6,873	7,581	10.3
Children < 18 Years						
No Children	24,853	27,755	11.7	11,989	14,256	18.9
One or more	26,987	30,256	12.1	9,721	12,395	27.5
All under 6	23,567	28,181	19.6	9,221	12,163	31.9
Some <6,some 6-17	26,175	29,564	12.9	8,216	10,732	30.6
All 6-17	29,010	31,636	9.1	10,394	13,067	25.8
Work Experience						
Full-time	27,329	30,606	12.0	13,692	16,603	21.3
Part-time	8,541	8,790	2.9	4,787	5,959	24.5
Years of school						
< 12 years	17,224	18,051	4.8	7,453	8,081	8.4
High school	23,702	24,483	3.3	9,868	11,373	15.2
College 1-3	26,833	29,179	8.7	11,687	13,872	18.7
4 years	34,169	38,973	14.1	13,347	17,599	31.9
5+ years	41,067	46,853	14.1	18,637	22,769	22.2

Source: U.S. Bureau of the Census (1991). Statistical Abstract of the United States: 1991 (111th ed.). Washington, DC.

1989a). The relative earnings of husbands and wives are closely related to their occupational distribution.

Occupations of Husbands and Wives

Despite a higher level of education, 45 percent of wives in dual-earner families were in either clerical or service occupations, the traditional bulwark of women's employment. An additional 30 percent of employed wives were in executive-managerial or professional-technical positions. Most of the remaining fourth were in sales or manufacturing (U.S. Department of Commerce, Bureau of the Census 1989a).

The largest share of wives were in clerical positions regardless of husband's occupation, except professional husbands, 38 percent of whose wives were also professional. Dual-earner husbands in manufacturing, service, and farming had wives primarily employed in service or clerical occupations. This is a manifestation of their joint education levels discussed above. Of those employed wives whose husbands were not employed, over half were evenly divided between clerical and service jobs, indicating the low level of education and earnings of these households.

The joint earnings of dual-earner couples by occupation of both husband and wife are shown in Table 3.11. Earnings of dual-earner couples averaged $39,488 in 1987, compared with $37,171 for all married-couple families. The dual-earners with over $60,000 in joint earnings were heavily concentrated among those with both husbands and wives who were executive-managerial or professional and those with executive-managerial husbands whose wives were in technical fields. These are the families often regarded as dual career, and their earning levels are closely related to the higher-education households described above. The lowest joint earnings, about $18,000, were for agricultural husbands whose wives were operators-fabricators or service. Dual-earner families are concentrated in middle and upper brackets of the earnings distribution. If income from all sources were included, total income would have been even higher for dual-earners.

SUMMARY AND CONCLUSIONS

There are fewer and fewer married couples in which the husband is the only earner, although husbands have consistently had a higher labor force attachment, higher earnings, and lower unemployment than all males. This family type has decreased in numbers and economic significance as dual-earners have increased. Approximately two-thirds of young married

Table 3.11

Mean Earnings of Married Couples by Occupations of Husband and Wife, 1987 (in dollars)

Husband's Occupation	All Married Couples	All Dual-Earners	Wife's Occupation						
			Exec, Mana-gerial	Profes-sional	Tech-nical	Sales	Admin. sup-port	Oper-ators	Ser-vice
Total	37,171	39,488	51,181	53,099	44,164	37,082	39,866	28,342	26,162
Executive, Managerial	53,627	55,058	60,251	67,037	63,405	54,154	50,329	37,588	37,594
Professional	53,383	55,520	65,916	60,311	54,647	54,503	50,039	38,658	37,729
Technical	42,257	44,493	53,628	50,851	45,172	n.a.	42,452	n.a.	36,094
Sales	43,562	45,927	58,521	53,880	46,988	42,553	44,409	33,553	32,973
Admin.Support	34,079	37,434	43,165	42,483	n.a.	35,843	38,433	31,392	26,805
Precision Production	32,571	35,651	43,035	42,842	38,836	33,173	38,086	30,889	28,456
Operators	28,725	32,198	38,141	40,240	36,592	29,925	35,483	29,412	26,676
Service	26,826	31,362	38,882	40,582	n.a.	27,151	35,103	24,392	24,686
Farming and Fishing	19,329	22,962	n.a.	36,529	n.a.	19,769	27,181	18553	17,962

Source: U.S. Bureau of the Census (1991). Statistical Abstract of the United States: 1991 (111th ed.). Washington, DC.

couples begin marriage with both partners employed, and most of these wives maintain their labor force attachment. One important result is that families are better protected against economic downswings and unemployment, since two workers provide greater economic security.

The 1960s was a pivotal period for change in family labor force participation and demographics. A long-term decline in the male labor force participation rate began, while that of wives began to increase more rapidly. The share of employed wives has continued to increase substantially for every age group and particularly for wives with children, whose employment status continues to shift from part-time to full-time. Most husbands of working wives are employed full-time, and the share of wives working full-time is increasing.

Dual-earner families have become an increasingly important segment of the population, and their economic impact is even greater than their numbers alone reveal. Compared with one-earner families, they are more educated, more mobile, higher income, more likely to be home owners, and bigger spenders. By 1991, median money income of dual-earner families was 55 percent greater than that of husband-only-earners. This income gap has widened over time in real income or purchasing power. One-earner family real income has changed little, while dual-earner real income continues to increase. The growth of dual-earner families has significantly affected the distribution of income. As they move into higher quartiles of the income distribution, one-earner families drop into the lower quartiles, increasing the degree of income inequality.

The role and position of dual-earners will continue to improve in relation to all households. These families will continue to move upward in the distribution of income, will set trends in consumer goods marketing, and will dominate the housing market. Their households, based on amenities, mobility, growing families, and demands for public goods, will drive private markets and public policy. The overall impact of increasing dual-earner families will stimulate and direct the economy.

4

Policy and Tax Responses to Dual-Earner Families

Major government policies, particularly those that embody income redistribution, such as taxes and subsidy payments, recognize the family as a single economic unit. Most of these policies are based on the marital status of households, whether they are recipients or payers. Because married couples receive special program and policy treatment, major questions of equity and efficiency arise, particularly for income tax and Social Security issues. For example, Social Security taxes are based on work status, while payments are based on either previous work status or marital status, so that these taxes are inequitable to dual-earner families.

Public policy that addresses family issues was historically designed for husband-only-earner families. While U.S. households have become increasingly diverse, the institutional response to this diversity has lagged the long-term demographic changes outlined in Chapter 3. Growth in the numbers and economic impact of dual-earner and other types of families ultimately generated some institutional reactions. Federal tax policies changed marginally, and over time, to address families with more than one earner, but Social Security policies have yet to deal with dual-earner families. Many other important family issues, such as reasonable availability of child care, have not received significant public policy response. However, one important policy change affecting families was the 1993 family leave legislation.

This chapter examines institutional response to changing families, with emphasis on the federal income tax and Social Security treatment of two-earner versus single-earner families. We present an overview of the impact of public policies, mainly taxes, on women's and wives' labor supply. The tax treatment of differently composed households and changes in the federal income tax are examined, followed by examples of simulated tax impacts on different types and compositions of families. The next section reviews the lack of response of Social Security policy to social change. In conclusion, we discuss alternative policies that might generate more equitable treatment of dual-earner families.

TAX POLICY AND WIVES' LABOR FORCE PARTICIPATION

The numerous factors influencing the participation of women and wives in the labor force have been widely analyzed in economic theory and empirical research. These factors are reviewed in chapters 2 and 3. Several classic economic studies describe household and personal characteristics affecting participation rates of women and wives (Mincer 1962; Becker 1965; Cain 1967). Other research studies focus on the influence of public policy on wives' decisions to work outside the home, most specifically on the impact of the federal income tax structure on women's labor supply (Rosen 1976a, 1976b, 1987; Quester 1977, 1979; Aaron 1987; Hausman and Poterba 1987; Rubin and Riney 1986; Rubin el al. 1987).

The effect of taxes and other opportunity costs on the labor supply of married women has become increasingly important. Net income, or spendable wage, rather than gross earnings, is a crucial determinant of wives' labor supply. The empirically observed income effect of the tax structure on wives' labor market decisions has been primarily a tax effect. Rosen (1976a, 1976b) presented thorough comparative reviews of earlier theoretical and empirical analyses of the decisions determining married women's labor force participation. His model provided a framework for investigating the extent of tax illusion. The major empirical conclusion was that married working women do not suffer from tax illusion and appear to react to tax rates in the rational manner assumed by standard economic theory. Quester (1977) found that wives responded to spendable wages (measured net of taxes and child care expenses) rather than gross wages, and that the inverse relationship between wives' hours worked and family income, exclusive of wife's earnings, was a tax effect. When women in professional and nonprofessional occupations were disaggregated, this general tax effect was reinforced (Quester 1979). Because wives make employment decisions by comparing after-tax wage and home productivity, Quester urged that the income tax structure be made both marriage-neutral and work-sector-neutral.

Wives' employment decisions are responsive to changes in the federal income tax structure, particularly in the marginal tax rate, deductions, and tax credits. For example, after its introduction the two-earner deduction increased the probability that a married woman would participate in the labor force. The effect of this deduction is stronger, the higher the deduction rate and the greater the after-tax income of the husband.

TAX TREATMENT OF DUAL-EARNER FAMILIES[1]

With the passage of the Revenue Act of 1942 the tax structure was transformed from a high-income-based levy to a broad-based one for most of the population. The following brief review of historical federal income tax treatment of one-earner and two-earner families provides a perspective on current dual-earner tax issues. Since 1948, the family has been the fundamental unit of income taxation. Under this tax structure the two incomes of husband and wife are summed and treated as one total household income. A marginal dollar of income earned by either spouse is taxed at the same rate. This practice has paramount influence on wives' labor force decisions.

Three major tax principles are advocated to ensure broad-based tax equity: progressivity or increasing marginal tax rates; households with equal incomes should pay equal taxes, other things being equal; and marriage neutrality of the system should be maintained (Levitan et al. 1988; Rosen 1992). An underlying issue is the difficulty of achieving these objectives simultaneously in a tax system. In fact, there are inherent conflicts that make it impossible to satisfy all three criteria with the same system. Family-related tax issues are particularly difficult to resolve because of the conflict between the goals of maintenance of progressivity and marriage neutrality in the tax structure (Hefferen 1982).

Marriage Neutrality

Marriage neutrality implies that the tax burdens of two individuals should not change when they marry. This is difficult for the dual-earner household to achieve when spouses' incomes are aggregated and a progressive income tax embodying increasing marginal tax rates is utilized.

Prior to 1948, personal income tax was independent of marital status. Marriage neutrality was not a problem because the individual tax schedule was used by most households. The 1948 introduction of income splitting changed the situation. Under that system, the joint tax liability of a married couple was computed as two times the tax on half their joint income. In states with community property laws dual-earner families had a tax advantage, whereby they could split the income, file separately, and utilize lower tax brackets. This afforded a tax subsidy to married couples. For example, under this income-splitting approach, a family with one income of $40,000 was taxed like two earners with $20,000 incomes. This was a distinct advantage under a progressive income tax system, and income taxes of a single person could be reduced when he or she married and maintained the same household income. In contrast, this advantage was not available in common-law states, where income was attributed to the individual who earned it. The 1948 Revenue Act, in effect, made all states community property states for income tax purposes. This eliminated one inequity but created other substantial inequities between the treatment of single individuals, one-earner, and dual-earner families. The result was that the tax bill of a single person could be as much as 40 percent higher than that of a married couple with an identical income, thus creating a singles' penalty (Quester 1979; Rosen 1987).

Marriage Penalty

In 1969 Congress responded to the singles' penalty by adjusting taxes so that a single taxpayer's liability could not be more than 20 percent higher than that of a married couple with the same taxable income. Since that time there has been a marriage tax that increases the joint federal income tax owed by employed couples when they marry and, particularly, by dual-earner families. While couples were not mandated to file joint returns, they faced higher tax rates if they filed separately than did single taxpayers. Thus, two-earner married couples faced a higher tax liability on a particular total income than did either one-earner married couples or single taxpayers with the same income.

The attempt to institute a marriage-neutral tax structure created a marriage tax for the two-earner household. For example, families with dual incomes over $25,000 and with the lower-income spouse earning more than 20 percent of the income, the penalties were very high. Two married workers each earning $25,000 could pay almost $3,000 more in taxes than one-earner families or single individuals at the same income level (Hefferen 1982). This situation prevailed until the 1981 tax reform legislation that decreased the tax liability of two-earner families.

In addition to reducing the marriage penalty, Congress has, for a number of years, aided working parents by permitting a tax credit for child care expenses. In 1980 a 20 percent credit for child care costs up to $2,000 for one child and $4,000 for two children was allowed, resulting in maximum credits of $400 and $800. The 1981 legislation increased this deduction, allowing dual-earner families with incomes below $10,000 a tax credit of 30 percent of child care cost up to $2,400 per child, with a maximum credit of $720 for one child and $1,440 for two children. The credit is reduced by 1 percent for each $2,000 additional income above $10,000, with a maximum credit of 20 percent for households with income of $30,000 or above.

Significant tax changes were implemented in the broad Economic Recovery Act of 1981. Marginal income tax rates were reduced by 3 to 11 percent from 1980 to 1983. This reduction had an impact on dual-earner families as well as all other households. An attempt to correct the marriage penalty was included with the marriage penalty deduction, which reduced the penalty of the progressive income tax on dual-earner families. For the first time, in 1982, married couples with two earners were allowed a 5 percent deduction of the lower-paid spouse's earnings, up to a maximum income of $30,000 per year, with a maximum deduction of $1,500. The deduction was increased to 10 percent in 1983, with a maximum deduction of $3,000. This marriage penalty deduction was repealed in the Tax Reform Act of 1986.

Tax Reform Act of 1986

The major tax reform act passed in 1986, during the second term of President Reagan, was considered by many to be the most important improvement in the tax system in decades. By greatly reducing deductions and opportunities for tax avoidance, this act plugged numerous tax loopholes and thereby permitted substantial reduction of marginal tax rates and increased standard deductions. The marginal tax rates were reduced to three levels—15, 28, and 33 percent of taxable income. The 1986 tax act did not change the tax credit for child and dependent care introduced in the 1981 law, which was one factor in favor of dual-earner families, but it did eliminate the two-earner deduction. Although the two-earner deduction was repealed, families with two earners were more likely than those with one earner to benefit from the lower marginal tax rates because they tended to have high incomes (Aaron 1987).

Under the 1986 law it was possible for marriage to lower the tax liability of a couple with just one earner, but taxes still increased if there were two earners with similar income levels; thus generalizations of its impact are difficult. The estimated net effect of the law was to provide a small tax advantage to couples with adjusted gross incomes lower than $30,000 and to retain a marriage penalty for higher earners (Levitan et al. 1988). The exact effect depended on the deductions allowed, or the number of dependents, and on the relative incomes earned by the two spouses. Spouses with widely divergent incomes received a marriage subsidy, while those with fairly equal incomes were penalized with a marriage tax (Rosen 1987).

By calculating simulations of the marriage penalty, Rosen (1987) concluded that the 1986 act probably reduced the dispersion of the marriage tax and lowered the average amount of the marriage penalty to $119. This relatively low figure conceals the more substantial $1,100 marriage tax paid by 40 percent of couples. The estimated average $609 marriage subsidy was received by about 53 percent of families (Rosen 1987). Thus, the overall effect of the 1986 tax law was by no means marriage-neutral.

The 1986 repeal of the dual-earner deduction, allowable since 1981, affected household net after-tax income and the employment decisions of wives. The elimination of this deduction reduced labor supply of the lower earner in the couple, but the marginal tax rate changes may have had offsetting effects. An increase of less than 1 percent in the labor supply was estimated for married men, while that for wives was larger. Most of this effect for wives was due to increased labor force participation rather than increased hours of work (Hausman and Poterba 1987). The net effect of the Tax Reform Act on wives' labor supply was relatively small.

Building on the 1986 Tax Reform Act, the 1990 Omnibus Budget Reconciliation Act incorporated more changes in the tax rate structure, raised the personal exemption and standard deductions, and reduced or eliminated numerous remaining deductions. After the substantial 1986 rate structure changes, the 1990 law introduced additional modifications, retaining only three tax brackets of 15, 28, and 31 percent. The first two brackets had increased maximum bounds compared with the previous rate schedule. However, the personal exemption and itemized deductions phaseouts introduced could lead to higher effective marginal tax rates for some families. No specific modifications were incorporated to address the potentially different tax burden of dual-earner families.

EXAMPLES OF TAX EFFECTS

The effects of changes in the 1986 and 1990 tax acts on married couples filing jointly, at different levels of income, are demonstrated in Table 4.1. Taxes paid by married couples at different earnings levels of both husband and wife have been calculated for 1982, 1987, and 1991, using the tax structure and the child care deduction for each year, and the marriage

Table 4.1
Estimated Impacts of Tax Changes on Married Couples,[a] 1982–1991

Husband's Earnings	Wife's Earnings	Taxes Paid			Percent Change	
		1982	1987	1991	1982–87	1987–91
No Children						
$15,000	$0	$1,443	$996	$750	-31	-25
15,000	10,000	3,637	2,496	2,250	-31	-10
15,000	15,000	5,023	3,246	3,000	-35	-8
30,000	0	5,023	3,246	3,000	-35	-8
30,000	15,000	10,365	6,723	5,380	-35	-20
30,000	20,000	12,425	8,123	6,780	-35	-17
30,000	30,000	16,825	11,444	9,580	-32	-16
50,000	0	12,425	8,123	6,780	-35	-17
50,000	20,000	21,625	14,944	12,380	-31	-17
50,000	35,000	28,975	20,194	16,580	-30	-18
50,000	50,000	36,449	25,529	21,016	-30	-18
Two Children[b]						
$15,000	$0	$350	$1,014	$1,785	-190	-76
15,000	10,000	1,827	486	165	-73	-66
15,000	15,000	3,195	1,262	915	-61	-27
30,000	0	3,195	1,262	915	-61	-27
30,000	15,000	8,337	4,245	3,165	-49	-25
30,000	20,000	10,297	5,645	4,136	-45	-27
30,000	30,000	14,697	8,700	6,936	-41	-20
50,000	0	10,297	5,645	4,136	-45	-27
50,000	20,000	19,397	12,200	9,736	-37	-20
50,000	35,000	26,747	17,450	13,936	-35	-20
50,000	50,000	34,201	24,114	18,243	-29	-24

[a]Calculations assume the standard deduction is applied in all cases.
[b]Calculations assume costs per child at a child care center = $1.50 per hour in 1982, $1.70 in 1987, and $1.75 in 1991.

penalty deduction last available in 1982. The effects of these tax changes, including child care deduction changes, determine the amount of taxes for each household.

In calculating annual household income taxes, we used the zero bracket amount for 1982 and the relevant standard deductions of $3,760 in 1987 and $5,700 in 1991. The personal exemptions of $1,000 for 1982, $1,900 for 1987, and $2,150 for 1991 were applied, with two exemptions for childless couples and four exemptions for couples with two children. In determining the child care deduction, average hourly child care costs for a child care center were used. These were $1.50 per child in 1982, $1.70 in 1987, and $1.75 in 1991 (Comparing Child-care Costs 1992). The calculations assume that there are no employer-provided dependent care benefits and that child care is purchased for all hours worked by a full-time-employed wife.

It is clear from Table 4.1 that the tax changes that occurred were beneficial for all the married-couple families with incomes ranging from $15,000 to $100,000, as taxes declined for these families during the 1980s. For those without children, taxes decreased about one-third from 1982 to 1987 at all income levels, but the declines were smaller between 1987 and 1991. The benefits of the tax changes were even larger for families with two children, due to the indexed personal exemptions and child care deductions. In these calculations, one-earner and dual-earner families at the same income level (for example, comparing a single earner making $50,000 with a husband earning $30,000 and a wife earning $20,000) have the same amount of taxes. In an alternative situation, comparing taxes of two single households with earnings of $30,000 and $20,000, their total taxes would be lower because each household would get the standard deduction, which is received only once by the married couple, whether there is one earner or two.

SOCIAL SECURITY AND DUAL-EARNER FAMILIES

Unlike the federal income tax, the Social Security system is funded by a payroll tax that gives no consideration to marital status. However, the Social Security benefit structure incorporates significant differences in the treatment of workers and households dependent upon marital status. Designed in 1935 for the single-earner family, Social Security generates substantial differences in the returns workers receive on their tax contributions, as exemplified by the contrasts in benefits between one- and two-earner families, and between singles and married couples. This section explores the lack of response by Social Security policymakers to social change and the fact that an important demographic shift toward dual-earner families has been ignored.

Social Security taxes on earned income are calculated using two criteria: the tax rate and the maximum amount of taxable income (the tax base). Since the inception of Social Security, both of these criteria have been consistently increased, so that the tax burden on workers has grown substantially. From the original tax rate of 1 percent on a tax base of $3,000 income, the rate has risen to 6.2 percent and the tax base to $57,600 in 1993. In addition, since Medicare was initiated in 1965, an additional tax for its funding has been imposed under Social Security. The Medicare rate is 1.45 percent on earned income up to $135,000. Thus, in 1993 the combined Social Security rate is 7.65 percent on the total earnings of over 80 percent of workers.

Social Security taxes are imposed on the earned income of each worker in the household up to the maximum tax base. For families with only one earner, only one tax is paid, but upon reaching retirement age the nonworking spouse is entitled to receive a payment equal to 50 percent of the working spouse's benefit, regardless of whether the worker is the husband or wife. This dependent benefit aspect of Social Security is a major, and perhaps the only, financial fringe benefit of nonworking spouses. However, for dual-earner families, Social Security taxes are imposed on both spouses' earnings, so total taxes paid may be much higher than for single-earner families.

When a spouse in a dual-earner household becomes eligible for Social Security benefits, he or she has the choice of collecting either his/her earned benefit or half of the spouse's earned benefit. For most retired wives who have been in the labor force, the 50 percent of the husband's benefit is higher than their own earned benefit, due to women's lower wages. For this reason, most dual-earner families do not benefit from the Social Security taxes paid by the working wife and receive no return on her contribution. In 1982 only 40 percent of ever-married women received benefits derived from their own work and contributions (Brown 1988). Even if the working wife receives Social Security benefits based on her own earnings record, wives get a low return from their mandatory tax contribution. The more extensive a wife's employment, the lower her return on the taxes paid compared with benefits she would have received as a nonemployed wife. It is the one-earner family that realizes the maximum return from its payments into the system (O'Neill 1981b; Blau and Ferber 1986; Brown 1988). Single workers subsidize families, and working wives may subsidize nonworking wives, with transfers from two-earner families and single individuals to multiperson families (Boskin 1986). Dual-earner families and singles are treated inequitably under the Social Security system because they are mandated to subsidize one-earner married-couple families.

Estimated Social Security taxes for married couples are shown in Table 4.2 for husbands and wives with different levels of income. The double Social Security taxation of dual-earner families is clear; both earners pay on their entire incomes up to $53,400 in these 1991 examples. For incomes below this cutoff level, the amount of taxes paid is the same on equivalent amounts of total household income regardless of the number of earners. For example, for one-earner families with income of $50,000 or dual-earners each of whom earns $25,000, the total household Social Security paid

Table 4.2
Estimated Social Security Taxes for Married-Couple Families, 1991

Husband's Earnings	Wife's Earnings	Estimated Social Security Tax[a]		
		Husband	Wife	Total Household
$15,000	$0[b]	$1,148	$0	$1,148
15,000	10,000	1,148	765	1,913
15,000	15,000	1,148	1,148	2,295
25,000	0	1,913	0	1,913
25,000	15,000	1,913	1,148	3,060
25,000	25,000	1,913	1,913	3,825
50,000	0	3,825	0	3,825
50,000	15,000	3,825	1,148	4,973
50,000	20,000	3,825	1,530	5,355
50,000	50,000	3,825	3,825	7,650
70,000	0	4,326	0	4,326
70,000	30,000	4,326	2,295	6,621
70,000	50,000	4,326	3,825	8,151
70,000	70,000	4,326	4,326	8,652

[a]1991 Social Security tax rate is total of 6.2% on income up to a maximum of $53,400 plus Medicare tax of 1.45% on income up to a maximum of $125,000.

[b]If wife's earnings = 0, then one-earner family case; other dual-earner cases assume that husband and wife are the only earners.

is $3,825. However, single earners at incomes above this cutoff benefit by lower taxes than if the household income were split between two earners. An example of this is seen for husbands with $70,000 incomes, who pay $4,326; but for a husband with $50,000 income whose wife earns an additional $20,000, total Social Security taxes are $5,355, over $1,000 more.

The Social Security tax inequity to dual-earners is magnified when the return on their tax dollars is considered, because of nonearning spouses' collection of benefits on the earning spouses' record. This is demonstrated in Table 4.3, which shows estimated Social Security benefits for one-earner and dual-earner couples. These data highlight two important facets of the redistribution of income through Social Security. First, benefits received are greater than lifetime payroll taxes only for low-income households, whether they are one-earner or dual-earner. Second, dual-earners pay greater taxes into the system than do single-earners at the same level of total family income, but their total expected benefits are lower for low- and middle-income families. In particular, the loss incurred by dual-earners with a $50,000 total earnings level ($109,691) is almost three

Table 4.3
Estimated Social Security Benefits[a] for Married-Couple Families, 1991

	Earnings Level		
	$10,000	**$30,000**	**$50,000**
One-Earner Family			
Social Security wealth	$62,679	$109,128	$100,503
Lifetime payroll taxes	48,951	136,498	140,253
Gain (loss)	13,727	(27,370)	(39,750)
Dual-Earner[b] Family			
Social Security wealth	53,293	96,044	108,428
Lifetime payroll taxes	48,264	144,760	218,119
Gain (loss)	5,029	(48,715)	(109,691)

[a]Calculations assume a real interest rate of 3 percent and that all individuals are born in 1945 and workers have 40 years in the labor force.
[b]The husband's earnings are twice the wife's.

Source: Boskin et al. (1986). Social Security: A Financial Appraisal across and within Generations. (Cambridge, MA: National Bureau of Economic Research), NBER Working Paper No. 1891, 19.

times the loss of a one-earner household with the same earnings ($39,750). The current Social Security system thus redistributes income from two-earner to one-earner couples, and from higher earners to lower earners.

CONCLUSIONS AND POLICY IMPLICATIONS

Both the federal income tax and Social Security systems favor nonworking wives and have inherent disincentives for wives' employment. The standard deduction applies only once to a household, regardless of the number of earners, but income is taxed at the margin on an additive basis. A basic element of horizontal equity—that those equally situated (i.e., making equal contributions to the system) should receive equal returns—is violated by Social Security in the case of dual-earner families. Despite these institutionalized disincentives to employment, wives have continued to enter and remain in the labor force. This discussion leads to the conclusion that changes need to be incorporated into our institutional structure to remove the financial disincentives to market work and to increase the horizontal equity of dual-earner families.

Taxes

Empirical studies have demonstrated that the net after-tax wage is the determining factor in a wife's decision to work. The major empirical conclusion is that married working women do not suffer from tax illusion and appear to react to tax rates and the tax structure with rational decision making (Rosen 1976a, 1976b). Assuming this to be so, then reduction of the income tax disincentives to working wives would potentially increase the number of dual-earner families and wives' motivation to maximize their earnings.

Several aspects of the tax system provide inequities or disincentives to the second household earner. The first of these is that only one standard deduction is allowed, which is the same regardless of the number of earners. The second is the fact that husband's and wife's earnings are additive when they file jointly; and the second earner is taxed on the first dollar of earnings at the highest marginal tax rate of the first earner. This ties a wife's marginal tax rate to her husband's income level. Both of these disincentives would be removed by permitting separate filing by married persons on the basis of their own earned income, and allowing each tax filer to claim the standard deduction. This would effectively put married taxpayers on the same footing as single taxpayers, and make the individual, rather than the family, the basic unit of taxation. Alternatively, married couples could retain the option of filing jointly or individually, whichever is more advantageous.

Another approach is the concept of income splitting. The rationale for this system is the assumption that "husbands and wives usually share their combined income equally" (Pechman 1989). Under this system (which was actually utilized from 1916 to 1969 in community property states, and from 1948 to 1969 in other states), the spouses would combine their income, split it in half, and each pay taxes on half, regardless of who earned the income. This system could also encompass one-earner married-couple families. Under income splitting, tax calculation on the reported income of each spouse would begin at the lowest tax rate. Either of these two tax modifications would remove the marriage penalty. However, both approaches would reduce total tax revenues and would increase administrative costs of cross-referencing and problems of investment shifting.

A third alternative would be to reinstate the marriage penalty deduction, which existed briefly during the 1980s. This deduction gave a special allowance to dual-earner families by allowing a deduction based on the earnings of the lower-earning spouse. This deduction was removed with the 1986 simplification of the tax rate schedule. Although these rate changes did reduce the inequities for spouses with unequal incomes, those with fairly equal incomes were penalized with a marriage tax, as discussed above.

While it is not possible to achieve complete equity for different households and maintain a progressive tax system, greater equity is possible. One approach would be to utilize income splitting, with the tax bracket also halved for married couples. A second is to reintroduce the marriage penalty deduction. This would shift more tax burden to one-earner families and away from single earners and two-earner families (Pechman 1989).

Social Security

The need to reform Social Security's treatment of the family has been widely recognized, but no changes have yet been made. The inequities in the treatment of dual-earner families need to be recognized and addressed in policy changes to reduce the forced subsidization of one-earner families by two-earner families. While it is highly unlikely that changes for older households would be politically feasible, reform of the system for younger workers, perhaps those under age forty, would be much more acceptable. Since these are the families with the greatest likelihood of wives' labor force participation, they will be the heaviest payers in the future and those most likely to benefit from policy changes.

An equitable approach for dual-earner families would be to phase out spousal benefits, which would have to be accomplished over an extended period. Then benefits would accrue only to workers, based on their own contributions, and the system would more closely approximate a compulsory pension system (O'Neill 1981b). This is the approach taken in some European countries, most notably in Switzerland, but those countries tend to have other support systems for nonearners.

Further, if this reform were instituted, the system could be extended to encompass nonmarket workers, who would pay Social Security taxes on the basis of a value attributed to their nonmarket work or alternatively, on the minimum wage contribution. Then these nonemployed spouses would have a claim to retirement benefits, regardless of divorce, death of spouse, length of marriage, or marital status. Such a plan would include nonemployed persons who are caregivers for other family members. This approach would replace potentially demeaning dependent's benefits with an individual benefit record. It would also require many current nonpayers to pay into the system against future benefits and generate additional revenue.

While the current Social Security system provides a financial disincentive to market work for married women, this proposal would, if made mandatory, obviate it. As wives' labor force participation and earnings increase, payment only on individual work records will become an increasingly viable alternative. Most of the current inequities would be resolved by these proposed changes, but many dependent persons would no longer have coverage.

An alternative approach to creating greater horizontal equity in Social Security payments for dual-earner families would be the institution of an earnings-sharing plan. Under such a plan, an earnings record would be created for each spouse based on total household earned income. The earnings of both spouses would be totaled and divided by two, so that each spouse would have an earnings record that reflected household earnings (O'Neill 1981b; Blau and Ferber 1986). This plan would acknowledge the homemaker or lower-earning spouse as an equal contributor to the marriage by monetizing the value of her or his contribution to the household. In the event of divorce, the lower-earning or nonearning spouse would gain, and the higher-earning spouse would lose, future benefits.

In sum, the present income tax and Social Security systems were developed in an era when one-earner families were the norm. Institutional responses to the vastly changed demographics of the American family have been very slow or, in the case of Social Security, nonexistent. These basic social policies discriminate against dual-earner families in several important respects. In so doing, they violate basic principles of horizontal equity in both tax and redistribution policies. Changes need to be made in both systems to mitigate their negative effects on working wives and to enhance the equitable treatment of different types of households.

NOTE

1. Portions of this section appeared in R. M. Rubin, B. J. Riney, and T. Johansen, Tax effects on the net income of wives in dual-earner households: 1980–1983, *Public Finance Quarterly* 15(4) (1987): 441–459.

5

Economic Effects of Wives' Employment

Increases in the labor force attachment of wives and in the number of dual-earner families have affected all aspects of household decision making. One of the crucial issues facing a family is determining the real benefits of the wife's employment. From an economic perspective, this includes effects on household production and consumption functions and effects on total after-tax income. Certain costs of working, most notably child care, are attributed to the wife's rather than the husband's employment, because most married men have consistently been in the labor force, while wives' participation has grown significantly only in recent decades (Chapter 3).

This chapter explores the major family economic issues related to wives' employment. The first section presents analyses of the impacts of wife's labor force participation on production and consumption theory. The next part is a discussion of the employment costs of wives, including work-related and household opportunity costs. Then we describe working wives' net economic contribution to household earnings, applying a cost-benefit model, the net earnings model, for families of differing incomes and compositions. Total family net income is assumed to consist of husband's after-tax earnings plus wife's after-tax earnings, minus the sum of the extra costs resulting from wife's employment. We present several examples of wives' net earnings for married-couple families of different compositions. The last section examines the social and policy implications of wives' employment for household production and net earnings. Issues of the social and psychological implications of wives' employment for the individual and the family are also very important, but these are beyond the scope of this study.

HOUSEHOLD PRODUCTION AND CONSUMPTION THEORY

Women's and wives' labor force participation decisions have been subjects of considerable interest in economic theory and empirical research (Chapter 2). According to Becker (1965), working wives place a higher marginal value on their time available for household work than do nonworking wives. Therefore, they will use more purchased goods (more market goods) in their household production function and spend more on labor-saving durables and appliances. More recent studies have analyzed the trade-offs between the labor force participation and household production functions of working wives. These studies imply that working-wife households have consumption and production functions different from those of nonemployed wives.

In household production theory, the consumption of goods and services yields satisfaction, or utility, for the members of the household. Utility (U) produced by consumption of the outputs (Z) generated by in-home production or purchased is specified as

$$U = u(Z). \tag{1}$$

The household production function describes the technology for combining commodities and household labor to produce goods and services for household consumption. It includes both purchased or market commodities and services and nonmarket goods and services produced by members of the household. While children or others in the household may contribute to household production, the following assumes that the labor inputs are provided by the husband and wife in a married-couple family. The household production function demonstrates the relationship between the various inputs used in production of goods and services and the resulting output available for household consumption (Z). It may be specified as

$$Z = f(W, H, C, I, M1, M2), \tag{2}$$

where

W = wife's contribution to housework and household services
H = husband's contribution to housework and household services

C = household capital (durable equipment and furnishings)
I = household inventory of nondurable goods
M1 = market purchases of goods
M2 = market purchases of services.

This household production function can be stated in a more measurable form as

$$Z_i = a + b_1 W_i + b_2 H_i + b_3 C_i + b_4 I_i + b_5 M1_i + b_6 M2_i + e, \tag{3}$$

where Z, W, H, C, I, M1, and M2 are as defined for equation 2 but are now applied to the *i*th household; a is an intercept whose level is determined by household tastes and preferences; e is an error term; and b_1, b_2, b_3, b_4, b_5, and b_6 are coefficients defining the level of contribution to household production of each input.

The input coefficients differ for an employed wife and a homemaker. These varying input combinations will result in a different output mix for consumption by the two types of households. When household income permits, the employed wife substitutes other goods and services for her labor or time inputs (specifically, b_1 generally decreases, while some or all of the other input coefficients increase). Thus, the output mix for the family is shifted toward increased consumption of purchased goods and services.

The output mix is selected by the family to maximize its joint or total utility, but total utility cannot be compared across families. Economic theory does not permit interpersonal or interfamily comparisons of utility, because utility has ordinal (but not cardinal) measurement. Therefore, we cannot conclude from their consumption or production functions that households with an employed wife are better off, because we cannot compare levels of utility.

Household total utility derived from consumption of the goods and services it produces cannot be equated with standard of living. The concept of a standard of living remains elusive in both theoretical and empirical terms. Lazear and Michael (1980) define the standard of living as the market value of the bundle of service flows consumed, expressible in dollar terms and allowing comparison across households. Brown (1987) defines this concept as including the well-being, comfort, and status of the household, which assumes that households evaluate their standard of living in comparison with their peer groups and their expectations. Thus, comparing standards of living across different types of households is difficult because nonquantifiable and subjective factors are included. This view is based on the writings of Davis (1945) and Cochrane and Bell (1956). The crucial difference between the market-based definition and the institutionalist view is the recognition of the family's social and institutional environment.

Although dual-earners average higher money incomes than single-earners, their standard of living as measured by Lazear and Michael (1980) may not be higher, due to the monetary and the time costs of employment. They found that although two-earner families had about 20 percent more money income after tax than comparable one-earner families, 30 percent more was required to have a similar standard of living. They attributed this to wife's decreased household production and work-related expenditures. The remainder of this chapter examines the financial impact of wife's employment on household spendable income.

COSTS OF WIFE'S EMPLOYMENT

Additional household income and costs are generated when a married woman is in the labor force. The important economic question for the family is how much incremental net earnings are realized from her employment, after all additional tax and other expenses. Numerous studies (Lazear and Michael 1980; Rubin and Riney 1986; Rubin et al. 1987) have analyzed net income contributions of wives in two-earner families by either real-income equivalence or spendable income. These studies emphasize the decrease in home services production and the increase in purchase of compensatory goods and services in the marketplace. Such shifts in home production technologies between one-earner and two-earner families represent opportunity costs of employment.

Wife's monetary contribution to the household is her net earnings after accounting for all costs related to employment and to changes in the household production/consumption function. These extra expenditures include additional taxes, work-related costs, and any extra out-of-pocket costs. We divide wives' employment costs into three categories: work-related, household-related, and those that generate employment benefits.

Work-Related Costs

Family net earnings are highly dependent upon the spouses' income levels because of the progressive income tax system. The highest cost of earning a second income in the family is the tax cost, including both federal income and Social Security taxes. The cost of child care is the second highest cost of employment. For lower-income families, this cost is partially offset by the income tax deduction for child care expenses.

Additional monetary costs are associated with wife's employment, including transportation and parking, work clothing, food at work, and miscellaneous out-of-pocket expenses. Salary deductions, such as union or professional dues and health and life insurance, also reduce net earnings. These vary widely between jobs and locations, and are difficult to estimate; thus they are not included in the examples calculated below.

Household Opportunity Costs

Household opportunity costs are the costs of goods and services purchased or forgone as a result of wife's employment. When alternatives are purchased, many opportunity costs of employment can be imputed from the market prices of comparable goods and services. Such costs include prepared food or food away from home, extra laundry services, additional household help, and any other items purchased as a substitute for wife's labor input. Higher-income dual-earners are likely to purchase alternative goods and services, while those with lower incomes either continue doing their own work or lower household standards. The latter is probably a common occurrence for many dual-employed families striving to increase earnings.

Costs of Employment Benefits

Employment costs (usually wage deductions) that establish claims to current and potential future benefits include payments into a retirement fund, insurance premiums, cafeteria or flex plan deductions, and Social Security taxes. Although these costs may be high, they generate potential benefits and are an important consideration in the employment decision, especially when subsidized by the employer's contribution. Short-term employment benefits include employer contributions to life and health insurance, travel allowances, discount purchasing, and other hidden income. Long-range benefits are primarily employer payments to Social Security, retirement, and pension funds. Long-range benefits are problematical to calculate and are not included in the determination of net earnings below. However, in the family life cycle these are among the most important benefits of wives' employment.

The concepts of work-related and household-related costs of employment are applied to examine wife's net earnings. A detailed model for the net earnings calculation in a dual-earner family is presented in the following section. It applies to the family's lower-income earner, who is effectively taxed at the highest marginal tax rate of the higher-income earner.

NET EARNINGS MODEL

The Net Earnings Model[1] (NEM) was developed by the authors to facilitate the calculation of net earnings in dual-earner families in which the earners are married and file joint federal income tax returns. This analysis considers only earned income (wages and salary) and not income from other sources. However, other income could be included, particularly since even capital gains are now taxed at the household's marginal tax rate. Further, the model does not attempt to encompass behavioral responses to changes in the tax regime. In the model, families utilize the standard federal income tax deduction rather than itemizing, and no contributions to Individual Retirement Accounts or other tax-sheltered annuities are made. This may introduce a bias into application of the NEM for higher-income households, which are more likely to itemize tax deductions and shelter income. These assumptions are more stringent the higher the dual-earner income.

The NEM has four structural groups of equations. Equations 1 through 8 calculate the effects of the federal income tax system on wife's income. Equations 9 through 17 calculate explicit costs of work and opportunity costs of forgone household production. Equations 18 through 20 determine current short-run fringe benefits of work and allow long-run benefits to be included. Equations 9, 21, and 22 utilize the products of these calculations to determine net earnings, net earnings as a percentage of salary, and wife's hourly net earnings. An overview of the model is presented in the chapter appendix, with the structural relationships specified in Table 5A.1.

The specification of the NEM below is based on the 1991 federal income tax code.

The combined gross income, CGI, of the two earners is

$$CGI = GI_1 + GI_2, \tag{1}$$

where GI_1 and GI_2 are the gross incomes of the first earner and spouse.

The adjusted gross income, AGI, of the household is

$$AGI = CGI - \text{adjustments}. \tag{2}$$

Dual-earner household taxable income, TAXI, is adjusted gross income less the personal exemption per family member

$$TAXI = AGI - (FSIZE \times PERSEXEM), \tag{3}$$

where FSIZE is the number of personal exemptions (PERSEXEM) claimed. FSIZE is two, if there are no children; and it is two plus the number of children for other cases. The model allows dependent children to be included in FSIZE as tax exemptions, whether or not they receive child care. For married couples filing jointly, TAXI is taxable income before the child care credit, CCRED.

$$CCRED = a \, CCC \text{ with } CCRED < \text{ or } = \$1,440, \tag{4}$$

where CCC is total child care cost for dependents under age fifteen, and a is a coefficient matrix of the percentage rates of child care cost tax credit, based on the amount of taxable income, TAXI. The child care cost is the total of costs incurred for all children in the family:

$$CCC = CCC_1 + CCC_2 + CCC_n, \tag{5}$$

where CCC_1 is child care cost for the first child, and CCC_2 is child care cost for the second child. CCC depends on the child care alternative selected by the household for each child.

$$CCC_i = HCR_i + HCNR_i + NS_i + DC_i, 66 \tag{6}$$

where HCR is annual cost of child care at home by relative, HCNR is cost at home by nonrelative, NS is cost at nursery school, and DC is cost of day care.

Therefore, the combined tax cost, CTC, for the dual-earner household with children is

$$CTC = TAX - CCRED, \tag{7}$$

where TAX is the amount of income tax calculated on joint taxable income, TAXI.

$$TAX = b \, TAXI, \tag{8}$$

where b is a coefficient matrix of married, filing jointly tax rates. Total joint income tax is used to calculate wife's net income, $NETI_2$:

$$NETI_2 = GI_2 - TAX_2 - WRC - HOC + TFB, \tag{9}$$

where GI_2 is wife's gross income, as in equation (1) above; TAX_2 is the calculated income tax on the second income; WRC is work related costs; HOC is household opportunity costs; and TFB designates wife's total fringe benefits.

Tax on wife's earnings, TAX_2, is calculated from the fact that the combined tax cost, CTC, in equation (7) above, is the sum of tax on the first income, TAX_1, plus tax on wife's earnings, TAX_2.

$$CTC = TAX_1 + TAX_2 \tag{10}$$

and

$$TAX_1 = b\ TAXI_1, \tag{11}$$

where $TAXI_1$ is husband's taxable income. Thus,

$$TAX_2 = CTC - TAX_1. \tag{12}$$

Work-related costs, WRC, of employed wives are

$$WRC = SSTAX + MEDTAX + TRANS + CLO + FOODW + DUES, \tag{13}$$

where SSTAX is Social Security taxes paid by the employee; MEDTAX is Medicare taxes; TRANS is the cost of private or public transportation; CLO is the cost of additional clothing necessitated for work; FOODW is the cost of food while at work; and DUES is union dues or other work-related costs.

$$SSTAX = d\ GI_2,\ \text{with}\ SSTAX < MAXSSTAX \tag{14}$$

$$MEDTAX = m\ GI_2\ \text{with}\ MEDTAX < MAXMEDTAX, \tag{15}$$

where d and m are the Social Security and the Medicare tax rates for the relevant year; MAXSSTAX is the maximum Social Security tax; and MAXMEDTAX is the maximum Medicare tax.

Transportation costs are

$$TRANS = (MILES \times CPM)\ DAYS, \tag{16}$$

where MILES is distance traveled, CPM is vehicle cost per mile, and DAYS is annual number of days worked.

Household opportunity costs (HOC) of wife's employment are expenditures to achieve at least the level of service flows that would exist if she were a full-time homemaker. These reflect different production technologies, incorporating increased market purchase of services.

$$HOC = CCC + XFOOD + XLDRY + XSERV, \qquad (17)$$

where CCC is child care cost; XFOOD is the cost of food eaten out or convenience food brought home; XLDRY is the cost of additional laundry generated by wife's employment or purchased; XSERV is the cost of additional household or other services purchased.

Total fringe benefits, TFB, of wife's labor force participation are added to net income. These include total current fringe benefits (TCFB) and total long-run benefits, TLRB:

$$TFB = TCFB + TLRB. \qquad (18)$$

Fringe benefits may include cash or in-kind benefits. Additionally, TLRB should be discounted to present values for inclusion in current value calculations.

$$TCFB = HEALTH + BONUS + XACCT + OTHER, \qquad (19)$$

where HEALTH is employer contribution to health insurance; BONUS is any bonus or gift; XACCT is employee expense account benefits; and OTHER includes miscellaneous perquisites.

$$TLRB = FICA_2 + FUND, \qquad (20)$$

where $FICA_2$ is employer contributions to Social Security and FUND is employer contributions to retirement. These benefits are important for the accrual of future income claims generated by current employment. An additional long-run benefit is the value of experience and on-the-job training, resulting in potential higher earnings in the future.

In addition to calculating wife's net earnings, this model calculates net earnings as a percentage of gross income, $NETI_2\%$, and wife's hourly net earnings, $HNETI_2$.

$$NETI_2\% = (NETI_2 \times 100)/GI_2 \qquad (21)$$
$$HNETI_2 = NETI_2/HOURS, \qquad (22)$$

where HOURS is hours of employment per year.

APPLICATIONS OF THE NET EARNINGS MODEL

The NEM is applied to develop simulations of wives' net earnings for different families. Distributions of the net earnings of full-time employed wives are calculated for a series of spouse income levels for families with no children and with one and two children requiring child care. These simulations, shown in Table 5.1, demonstrate the differences between wives' earnings and their net additions to household spendable income.

For most wives without child care expenses, taxes are the highest cost of employment, due to the additive effect of the progressive income tax system on the dual-earner family. The simulations in Table 5.1 use 1991 tax rates, with a personal exemption of $2,150 per individual in the family and a standard deduction of $5,700. An inequity in the tax system is that dual-earner couples filing jointly get only one standard deduction. Since the 1981 Tax Act, working couples with one or more children in paid child care are entitled to a child care credit, the amount of which is dependent upon child care costs and the level of combined income (see Chapter 4). Dual-earners are eligible for a maximum tax credit of $720 for one child and $1,440 for two children, depending on their income level.

In addition to increased taxes, working wives encounter a range of other costs generated by their employment. We functionally separate these costs of earning the second household income into work-related costs and household opportunity costs, as described above. Work-related costs include Social Security taxes, transportation, clothing, and food at work. The Social Security taxes for the earnings levels in Table 5.1 are shown in Table 4.2. For very low earners, Social Security taxes may be higher than federal income taxes.

The work-related costs of transportation, clothing, and food at work are marginal work costs used in the calculations reported in Table 5.1. Since the vast majority of workers in this country use automobile transportation, we assume that the wife travels to work by car. The U.S. average distance to work is 12.1 miles, a daily journey of 24.2 miles, and we assume this average mileage for wives (U.S. Federal Highway Administration 1992). The U.S. Bureau of the Census (1992) reports that the average cost of owning and operating an automobile is 32 cents per mile (including depreciation, maintenance, gas, and oil), so annual work transportation costs are $1,936. We assume parking is provided by the employer and no additional parking costs or tolls are incurred.

Previous studies (Strober 1977; Guadagno 1990) have found that wives' clothing expenditures in one-earner and two-earner families are not significantly different, and in some cases marginal expenditure is larger for

Table 5.1
Estimated[a] Net Earnings of Wives in Dual-Earner Families, 1991

Husband's Earnings	Wife's Earnings	Wife's Net Earnings					
		No Children		One Child		Two Children	
		Amount	Percent[b]	Amount	Percent[b]	Amount	Percent[b]
$15,000	$10,000	$5,049	50	$2,989	30	$(511)	-5
15,000	15,000	8,917	59	6,857	46	3,357	22
30,000	15,000	8,787	59	6,857	46	3,357	22
30,000	20,000	12,004	60	10,224	51	7,003	35
30,000	30,000	18,439	61	16,659	56	13,438	45
50,000	20,000	10,184	51	8,124	41	4,624	23
50,000	35,000	19,837	57	17,777	51	14,277	41
50,000	50,000	29,254	59	27,258	55	23,823	48
70,000	30,000	16,384	55	14,388	48	10,953	37
70,000	50,000	28,654	57	26,658	53	23,223	46
70,000	70,000	41,897	60	39,901	57	36,466	52

[a]Net earnings calculated using the Net Earnings Model.
[b]Wife's net earnings as a percent of wife's total earnings.

nonemployed wives (Jacobs et al. 1989). Therefore, our calculations do not include a marginal clothing cost. Few data are available for determining wives' cost of food at work, so a conservative estimate of $3.00 per day (an annual total of $750) was assumed, regardless of income level. Although we recognize that these expenditures are likely to vary with occupation, income level, and household size, we assume constant values (except for Social Security) due to lack of empirical data providing cost distributions. Calculations of wives' total work-related costs ranged from $3,451 to $7,068, with this variation due solely to Social Security taxes.

In addition to work-related costs, most dual-earners find their household production function changed from its one-earner form. Household opportunity costs, most of which are homemaker services forgone, are imputed from the market prices of comparable purchased services. They vary among households, depending upon income level, family composition, and tastes and preferences. These expenditures rise with income for both one-earner and dual-earner families, so the difference in expenditures at the same income level is not as great as might be expected (Jacobs et al. 1988; Soberon-Ferrer and Dardis 1991).

Child care costs are the highest household opportunity cost and second only to taxes in total opportunity costs. The cost of child care is a major work disincentive for families, and may motivate wives to seek part-time employment or otherwise impact their job selection. Jacobs et al. (1988) found that working wives spend an average of 17 to 18 percent more on child care annually. The cost of child care averaged $1.75 per hour at a child care center in 1991 (Comparing Child-Care Costs 1992), so $3,500 is the annual cost used in Table 5.1 for one child of full-time dual-earners working fifty weeks a year. In this example we use the same amount for each child, although some day care centers give discounts for additional children in the family (Bane 1979).

Other household opportunity costs, such as prepared foods, laundry services, and household help, were not included in our calculations because empirical data are lacking. These expenditures are highly variable over the distribution of dual-earner incomes (Schwenk 1989) and vary with full-time or part-time employment (Soberon-Ferrer and Dardis 1991). If empirically derived opportunity cost distributions were available, these costs would further reduce wives' net earnings.

These tax and cost data were used to compute wives' net earnings and net earnings as a percent of earnings, by number of children (Table 5.1). The inverse effect of husband's earnings level on wife's net earnings is the most obvious result, with the impact of child care costs second. We emphasize the case with husband's earnings of $30,000 and wife's earnings of $20,000, because the 1991 median income of dual-earner families was $48,742 (U.S. Bureau of the Census 1991). In this case, wife's net earnings are $12,004, $10,224, and $7,003, with no children, one child, and two children, respectively. Wife's net earnings as a percent of her earnings are 60 percent, 51 percent, and 35 percent for these three family sizes. This comparison illustrates the substantial impact of federal taxes and child care costs on net earnings, with limited other costs included.

The decline in wife's net earnings with children occurs despite the tax exemptions of added family members and the child care credit. However, the rate of decline slows as spouse's income increases for two reasons. First, by assumption, the deductions from the wife's income do not change with higher household gross income, and second, by law, the maximum marginal tax rate is reached. Thus, two important caveats must be recognized. Household cost data may vary from the estimates incorporated here. Also, at higher levels of total family income and tax brackets, there is greater incentive to increase tax deductions and to shelter income with IRAs, tax-sheltered annuities, investment in real estate including a home, and other mechanisms. It is unlikely that married women with high-income spouses would find their net incomes actually reduced to the levels shown. The data, therefore, overstate the expected decline in net earnings of dual-earner families at higher income levels although only a limited number of work expenses are included. The NEM allows calculation of family net earnings, using the format in the appendix to this chapter.

If some arbitrary decision criterion is imposed on the data, then whether wife's employment pays becomes apparent. For example, if net earnings equal at least 25 percent, then the decision would be to work in all cases for childless families or those with one child, based on the data in Table 5.1. But for those with two children in day care, the wife would work only if family earnings approached the median ($45,747 in 1992). Otherwise, for low-earning wives with two children the economic decision would be withdrawal from the labor force. An important exception to this rational decision occurs in the case of a very-low-income family, where any addition to total income improves the financial situation. For these families informal substitutes take the place of formal child care, which is not affordable.

An alternative decision criterion is to work if net earnings are at least minimum wage ($4.35 per hour). In this case, our calculations show that with husband earning $15,000, a wife earning $10,000 will net only $2.42 with no children and $1.49 with one child; but with two children she will spend $.26 per hour more than her earnings. Thus, in dual-earner families with no children where each spouse earns $15,000, the wife nets more than minimum wage ($4.46). With husband earning $30,000 and one child, the wife must earn approximately $20,000 to net at least minimum wage; and with two children, she must earn closer to $30,000. Thus, the criterion applied and the weight allotted to nonincome factors determine the family's decision.

CONCLUSIONS AND POLICY IMPLICATIONS

These analyses demonstrate the applicability of the Net Earnings Model as a decision-making tool both for dual-earner families and for societal policymaking. For dual-earners the two critical determinants are their joint earnings level, which establishes their tax bracket, and the presence of young children requiring child care.

Our findings raise the issue of why many married women enter the labor force or continue to work when the net monetary returns seem so low, since previous research demonstrated that working wives make labor force decisions utilizing net income. They may consider the importance of experience and potential future higher earnings or the long-term benefits or pensions. They may be responding to perceived social pressure to be in the labor force. Wives may recognize that their family situation is subject to change and they could become the sole support of their children.

This study implicitly emphasizes the distinction between taxable income and nontaxable income (fringe benefits) for employed wives, since nontaxable benefits or in-kind income may generate greater returns than wage raises. This situation may change, however, if the present thrust of tax reform is enacted, and the nontaxable status of fringes is reduced, especially for employer-sponsored health insurance. The high opportunity costs of married women workers indicate that business policy innovations promoting family considerations may be cost effective. These policies include flextime to minimize child care costs and utilization of work-at-home techniques, such as employee home computers.

Our analysis of dual-earner families has a variety of societal and public policy implications. The crucial role of taxes and the tax structure in wives' net earnings is emphasized. Although the marriage penalty tax deduction, which existed from 1982 to 1986, provided only partial reduction of tax inequities for dual-earners, it did help many households. A substantial marriage tax penalty exists, and removal of this inequity will provide greater work incentives for dual-earners.

Public policymaking has largely failed to recognize the importance of dual-earner families as a factor that reduces the impact of adverse macroeconomic conditions. For example, when recession-induced unemployment peaked in late 1982, over 11 million persons were jobless, with nearly 10 million of them living in families. In two-thirds of these families, there was another worker, which was a major factor in cushioning the effect of unemployment on family income (Norwood 1984). An important incentive for having two earners may be to cushion the effects of potential unemployment on the family. However, given the low net monetary returns for most working wives, a considerable research agenda remains to rationalize their labor force participation.

NOTE

1. The NEM was published in R. M. Rubin and B. J. Riney, Second earner net income model and simulated income distributions for dual earner households, *Social Science Quarterly* 67(2) (1986): 432–441. The model was applied in R. M. Rubin, B. J. Riney, and T. Johansen, Tax effects on the net income of wives in dual-earner households: 1980–1983, *Public Finance Quarterly* 15(4) (1987): 441–459.

APPENDIX

Table 5A.1
Net Earnings Model, 1991

---

(1) $CGI = GI_1 + GI_2$

(2) $AGI = CGI -$ adjustments

(3) $TAXI = AGI - (FSIZE \times 2150)$

(4) $CCRED = a\ CCC$, with $CCRED <$ or $= \$1,440$

(5) $CCC = CCC1 + CCC2 + CCC_n$

(6) $CCC_i = HCR_i + HCNR_i + NS_i + DC_i$

(7) $CTC = TAX - CCRED$

(8) $TAX = b\ TAXI$

(9) $NETI_2 = GI_2 - TAX_2 - WRC - HOC + TFB$

(10) $CTC = TAX_1 + TAX_2$

(11) $TAX_1 = b\ TAX_1$

(12) $TAX_2 = CTC - TAX_1$

(13) $WRC = SSTAX + MEDTAX + TRANS + CLO + FOODW + DUES$

(14) $SSTAX = .062\ GI_2$, with $SSTAX <$ or $= \$3,366.60$

(15) $MEDTAX = .0145\ GI_2$ with $MEDTAX <$ or $= \$1,812.50$

(16) $TRANS = (MILES \times CPM)\ DAYS$

(17) $HOC = CCC + XFOOD + XLDRY + XSERV$

(18) $TFB = TCFB + TLRB$

(19) $TCFB = HEALTH + BONUS + XACCT + OTHER$

(20) $TLRB = FICA_2 + FUND$

(21) $NETI_2\% = (NETI_2 \times 100) / GI_2$

(22) $HNETI_2 = NETI_2 / HOURS$

Source: R. M. Rubin and B. J. Riney (1986). Second Earner Net Income Model and Simulated Income Distributions for Dual-Earner Households. *Social Science Quarterly 67(2), 432–441*

Table 5A.2
Calculation of Net Earnings in Dual-Earner Families, 1991

A. FEDERAL INCOME TAX EFFECTS ON 2ND EARNER
    (Married Filing Jointly)

    1. Earnings of 1st earner $_____
    2. Earnings of 2nd earner   _____
    3. Combined earnings   _____
    4. Adjusted gross income   _____
    5. Personal exemptions (-$2,150 per)_____
    6. Standard deduction (-$5,700)   _____
    7. Taxable income   _____
    8. Tax before child care credit   _____
    9. Child care credit (-)   _____
  10. Household taxes (on both incomes)_____
  11. Tax based on 1st income (-)   _____

  12. TAX COST of 2ND INCOME $_____

B. MARGINAL MONETARY COSTS OF 2ND EARNER

    1. Work related costs: Amount
        a. FICA (Social Security) $_____
            (7.65% on income up to $54,300 per earner)
        b. Transportation & parking   _____
        c. Additional clothing   _____
        d. Food away from home   _____
        e. Union/profession dues   _____
        f. Retirement fund   _____
        g. Other (specify)   _____

    TOTAL WORK RELATED COSTS $_____

    2. Opportunity cost of homemaker's services
        (some may be imputed)
                           Amount
        a. child care $_____
        b. Prepared food or
            food eaten out   _____
        c. extra laundry   _____
        d. household help (hired)   _____
        e. consumer search time   _____
        f. yard help (hired)   _____
        g. record keeping   _____
        h. Other: _____   _____

    TOTAL HOME OPPORTUNITY COSTS $_____

    3. TOTAL COSTS OF 2ND EARNER $_____

    4. NET EARNINGS OF 2ND EARNER $_____

Table 5A.2 (Continued)

C. MONETARY BENEFITS OF 2ND EARNER

   1. Current monetary benefits: Amount

      a. Employer contribution
          to health insurance $_____
      b. Bonuses/gifts/travel   _____
      c. Expense account   _____
      d. Transportation/food, etc.   _____
      e. Other: _____   _____

      TOTAL MONETARY BENEFITS $_____

   2. Long range benefits:

     a. Employer contribution to Social Security $_____
     b. Employer contribution to retirement fund   _____
     c. Other: _____   _____

      TOTAL LONG RANGE BENEFITS $_____

D. NET EARNINGS OF 2ND EARNER

   a) Net earnings of 2nd income $_____

   b) Net earnings as a percentage of 2nd income _____%

   c) Net earnings per hour $_____

6

Expenditures of Married-Couple Families

A major impact of dual-earner families on the economy is the strength of their spending power. By 1987, married-couple families had annual consumption of $840 billion (Waldrop 1989). The economic impact of dual-earner families is measured by the divergence of their expenditures from those of other households. Since wife's employment affects family lifestyle and consumption, we expect patterns of expenditures to differ between one-earner and two-earner families. For example, will the family bake its own bread, purchase sliced bread, or eat in a restaurant? This chapter examines these decisions through analyses of household expenditures by wife's employment status.

The transformation in women's work roles raises numerous important questions of household decision making about income, household production and consumption, expenditure patterns, and family size and child care. First, we distinguish among the concepts of consumption, expenditures, and standard of living. An analysis of the demographic variables that influence family spending follows. We next compare previous studies of detailed expenditure patterns of one- and two-earner families, by major expenditure categories. In the last section, providing a discussion of our two empirical studies, we use data from the Consumer Expenditure Survey (CE) to show differences in expenditures between types of families by wife's work status.

CONSUMPTION AND EXPENDITURES

Twentieth-century changes in expenditure patterns, especially for food and transportation, and changes in technology, family size, and women's education levels have freed wives from some household demands and facilitated their employment. Several theories examine the relationship between household consumption norms and wives' labor force participation. The dominant view derives from Mincer-type labor supply models emphasizing wife's employment decision making in the context of intra-family trade-offs. An alternative theory stresses that the shift to new consumption patterns allowed increasing numbers of wives to participate in the labor force (Brown 1987). These approaches differ from Veblen's much earlier theory of conspicuous consumption, which perceived wives' consumption of leisure as the indicator of social standing (Veblen 1899; Carter 1987). In strong contrast to Veblen, we now see increased consumption of purchased goods and services superseding leisure as symbolic of social standing.

Although money income is higher, the two-earner family may not have a higher standard of living than its single-earner counterpart (Lazear and Michael 1980). Money income is transformed into service flows or potential consumption differently in these two family types. This results primarily from taxes, different household production functions, and the costs of earning the second income. As discussed in Chapter 5, taxes and work costs are deducted from income to compare levels of living; but different household production functions, implicit within the household technology, are not comparable. The changing perception of family standards of living over time has affected expenditure patterns. As the importance of necessities decreased in family budgets, household expenditures on goods and services that promote social interaction and greater financial security—transportation, recreation, and insurance—increased.

Most researchers examine expenditures, rather than consumption, because numerous factors other than current spending affect household consumption. The Consumer Expenditure Survey data reflect current expenditures, without adjustment for the contribution of durables to household consumption or for the estimation of current-year depreciation (Fareed and Riggs 1982; Danziger et al. 1982). Also, expenditures in the CE data reflect their price at time of purchase, even if they are financed over time. Interest payments, whether on mortgages or on short-term financing, represent current spending that does not translate into consumption.

For those families living in an owner-occupied home without a mortgage, no housing payments indicate consumption of shelter, or the flow of services from their home. Further, many households have inventories of durable goods that are used for current consumption but do not reflect current expenditure. CE expenditures include some items that do not represent current consumption, such as life insurance, Social Security deductions, gifts, and donations. In addition, family consumption includes some items that are not purchased, such as gifts to the family, employment fringe benefits, and medical care paid by insurance. Therefore, in any period a family's consumption may be larger or smaller than its expenditures.

DEMOGRAPHIC DETERMINANTS OF FAMILY SPENDING

While household expenditures and consumption norms are determined primarily by income, demographic characteristics of the family are also important determinants of spending. Most expenditure studies explore how certain demographic variables affect household decisions. Microeconomic theory tends to assume that tastes and preferences determine differences in decision making on the demand side of the market. When tastes and preferences are assumed or taken as given, then the predictive power of the theory is reduced. This is countered by emphasizing the impact of various demographic variables on the income and expenditure of households (Ketkar and Cho 1982). The demographics most often cited are education level, family size, age of householder (representative of life-cycle stage), work status of spouse, geographic location, and home ownership.

The education level of family members determines the value of time and its opportunity cost. Increases in wives' educational level alter expenditure patterns, with increased emphasis on purchase of market-produced goods and services. One empirical study emphasizing the impact of wife's education on family spending found that it influenced all expenditures except food and housefurnishings and equipment (Abdel-Ghany and Foster 1982). Wives' valuation of their time strongly affects the home production model and technologies used, as well as the goods and services purchased to substitute for the inputs of time and labor. As wife's time becomes more expensive, home production becomes less time-intensive (Ketkar and Cho 1982). Home production time becomes relatively more valuable in relation to other commodities in dual-earner compared with one-earner families (Jacobs et al. 1989).

The variables of family size and age and the concept of family life cycle are closely related, with younger households likely to be larger. Family size is larger for one-earner than for dual-earner households, regardless of income. The expenditure effects of family size are less obvious than might be expected, since they also depend on age of children. In particular, families with children under age six tend to reallocate expenditure toward child care and domestic services (Bellante and Foster 1984). Intrafamily transfers of spending also affect spending patterns, with adults forgoing some expenditures in favor of the children. Only if very detailed expenditures are examined for specific categories, such as clothing, does this become apparent.

Age of householder is often a proxy for distinct life-cycle effects. Younger households are usually assumed in the family formation and borrowing stage, increasing their inventories; households of middle age are viewed as drawing on their inventories and increasing financial security; and older households have usually withdrawn from the labor force and have increased health expenditures. Life-cycle stage also impacts housing needs and expenditures.

Wife's labor force participation is a major demographic agent of change and the focus of much research effort. The interrelationship between wife's employment and family expenditure patterns varies with full- or part-time work status. Studies that do not control for other demographic variables (such as education, age, and race) may erroneously attribute additional explanatory power to employment status rather than its determinants (Bellante and Foster 1984).

Home ownership is used less often as an explanatory variable of expenditure differences between types of families, but this exclusion may induce some research bias. In recent decades, housing expenditures have replaced food as the largest share of family spending. Housing encompasses one-fourth to one-half of household expenditures, with the average married couple spending about one-third on housing; and the most affluent families with employed wives spend the most on housing (Waldrop 1989). Housing is a dominant factor in the household's perception of its relationship to its peer group, so the desire for home ownership may be a major motivating factor in wife's employment decision and commitment to the labor force (Jacobs et al. 1989). Federal law has mandated that wife's earnings be included in the household income base for home mortgage consideration. In addition, home ownership is positively correlated with service expenditures, implying complimentarity between home ownership and the purchase of time-saving services (Bellante and Foster 1984). The following section examines the impacts of these demographic variables on trends in expenditures by dual-earner families.

EXPENDITURES OF DUAL-EARNER FAMILIES

Since employment decreases wife's time for either leisure or housework, a broad assumption is that the family purchases more goods and especially services. Previous researchers hypothesized that families will increase expenditures for convenience foods, time-saving durables, and services because of employed wives' time constraints. Dual-earner families are expected to spend significantly more on those categories related to the opportunity costs of wife's employment. However, comparison of empirical studies of expenditure differences between one-earner and dual-earner families reveals mixed findings or relatively small differences, unless the researchers use highly disaggregated data. Some differences were found in these cases based on occupational status or comparisons across income levels. We present the major findings of numerous studies, looking at expenditures on durables, services, and other work-related expenses of wives, including food, transportation, and clothing.

Durables

As a result of Becker's (1965) time allocation theory, the relationship between wives' employment and household expenditures has received considerable attention, particularly durables purchases. Utilizing 1968 data from the Survey of Consumer Finances, researchers analyzed the substitution of capital equipment for wives' nonmarket labor by examining durables expenditures of one- and two-earner families with the quantity and quality of household production held constant (Strober 1977; Strober and Weinberg 1977, 1980). When income, assets, and other variables were held constant, there were no significant differences between expenditures by the two types of families for durables (including dishwasher, dryer, refrigerator, stove, washer, TV, furniture, and microwave oven). Wives' labor force behavior did not determine household purchase decisions or size of expenditure for durables. Once we account for the impact of wives' earnings on family income, working-wife families have the same spending patterns as other households on major durable goods. Although employed wives report a time shortage, regardless of household income level or life-cycle stage, the differences in the purchase of time-saving durables between the two groups are limited.

Others studied the influence of wife's employment on expenditures for labor-saving appliances, using either the Consumer Expenditure Survey or the Survey of Consumer Credit (Foster et al. 1981; Reilly 1982; Weinberg and Winer 1983). Their findings reinforced the previous studies' finding that total family income is the critical determinant of durables ownership. A study of role overload and convenience consumption of time-saving durables further supports these findings (Reilly 1982).

Overall, these studies of durables expenditures found that family income level had more influence on expenditures than the number of hours wives worked or other variables. When wives' contribution to household income is held constant, dual-earner families do not spend differently for durables than single-earner families. While these studies focused on particular labor-saving durables, analysis of the relationship between wives' employment and total durables expenditures showed contrasting results, using aggregated durables expenditures from the 1977–1978 Survey of Consumer Credit (Bryant 1988). Wives' time and durables were complements rather than substitutes, the premise of most previous studies.

Services

The expectation that working-wife families purchase more services is another underlying research assumption. Household expenditure differences for child care and other household services are examined in numerous studies. Child care is the major family opportunity cost of dual-earner employment. Child care expenditures in the CE data include day care, baby-sitting, nursery school, and other care. There is a clear consensus of findings that dual-earner families spend significantly more on child care than one-earner families, whether the wife works full- or part-time (Nickols and Fox 1983; Bellante and Foster 1984; Jacobs et al. 1989; Yang and Magrabi 1989). Others found significant differences between families with full- and part-time working wives (Soberon-Ferrer and Dardis 1991). For older children the difference narrows, with expenditure for children under age twelve significantly larger than for those over twelve (Jacobs et al. 1989). We found few families with three or more children under age six among dual-earner households.

Household services other than child care include domestic services, clothing care, and personal care. In two earlier studies that utilized limited demographic independent variables, two-earner families spent more than one-earner families on domestic and household services (Waldman and Jacobs 1978; Vickery 1979). While the number of weeks worked has some impact on expenditures for food-away-from-home and child care, this factor does not impact domestic services, or personal care and clothing care when other demographic variables are controlled (Bellante and Foster 1984; Soberon-Ferrer and Dardis 1991). Wife's work status does not significantly influence purchases of personal care services (Foster 1988) or domestic services (Yang and Magrabi 1989), but families with full-time employed wives purchase more total services (Soberon-Ferrer and Dardis 1991).

The finding that working wives do not use more domestic services than nonemployed wives is notable. It suggests that differences in household production functions between the two types of families derive more from internal family substitution than replacement of wives' housework with purchased services. It may be that employed wives reduce their leisure time, or that household standards are reduced and less housework is done, or it may be done by other family members.

Work-Related Expenses

Other work-related expenditures that may be higher for employed wives include food, transportation, and wife's clothing for work.

Food. Food expenditure is categorized as food-at-home, food-away-from-home, and convenience or prepared foods. If Becker's (1965) theory of time allocation is relevant to the purchase and preparation of food, then employed wives will have larger expenditures on food-away-from-home and convenience foods. However, analyses of this relationship have mixed results, probably due to changing eating habits of all families.

Purchase of food-away-from-home has grown steadily for all households, increasing almost 5 percent annually in the decade before 1980, when it was one-third of the average food budget (Brown 1987). The full- or part-time work status of the wife is a determining factor in the purchase of food-away-from-home. Families of part-time working wives do not spend significantly more on food-away-from-home, but families of wives employed full-time do (Bellante and Foster 1984). Based on more recent CE data, work status of both full- and part-time employed wives positively affects purchase of food-away-from-home (Foster 1988). For meals at restaurants, there were no significant differences between full-time-employed- and nonemployed-wife families. However, families of part-time working wives spend less at restaurants than those with full-time working wives (Yang and Magrabi 1989). This contrast may depend on household income level more than eating preferences, because when income level is held constant, the budget share spent on food-away-from-home is not correlated with the number of weeks a wife works (Waldman and Jacobs 1978).

When wives are newly entered into the labor force, their families spend more on food-away-from-home than when they are full-time homemakers. Not only are these wives likely to purchase breakfast or lunch at work, but their families are more likely to eat dinner out. Overall, the food-away-from-home expenditures of working-wife families are only 2 to 3 percent higher than those of one-earner families, which again is a reflection of income level rather than just wife's work status (Jacobs et al. 1989).

Full-time homemakers have greater expenditure than employed wives for food-at-home (Rubin et al. 1990), which may reflect more time spent in food preparation or the use of more expensive food items. There is no significant difference between wife's work status and household purchase of convenience foods (Strober and Weinberg 1980), which we find contrary to the expectations from time allocation theory. This is a further indication that all families utilize newer prepared food products. The mixed findings of these studies of food consumption may relate to the use of different data sources, but they nonetheless indicate that over time, wife's employment status is becoming a less distinctive determinant of household food consumption.

Transportation. Transportation expenditures reflect the fixed cost of automobile ownership, as well as current vehicle purchases, and the variable costs of operation. Since most expenditure data is from the Consumer Expenditure Survey, its treatment of these components is important. Vehicle purchases are large, infrequent expenditures that are likely to be financed, but they (like all purchases) are included in the CE data at their total purchase price, regardless of the mode of financing. Therefore, purchase of vehicles is an item that can skew average transportation expenditures.

New and used vehicle purchase and public transportation expenditures are the same for both dual- and single-earner families (Jacobs et al. 1989). However, since dual-earner families own more vehicles than one-earner families, operating costs for oil and gas are higher for both full- and part-time working-wife households. Part-time employed wives do not increase their time spent carpooling or the use of public transport to reduce transportation costs (Foster 1988).

Clothing. To analyze the impact of wife's work status on clothing expenditures, only purchases of clothing for work apply. Wife's employment significantly affects expenditures for all women's clothing, whether work-related or not (Nelson 1989). Full-time working wives spend more on their apparel than nonemployed wives, but the difference declines with age; and after age twenty-four, part-time working wives also spend more on clothing than nonworking wives (Jacobs et al. 1989). These age differences probably reflect the more extensive wardrobes accumulated by older employed wives. When wife's occupation is considered, wives in white-collar occupations have higher clothing expenditures than those in blue-collar occupations (Norum 1989). Wives employed in the three occupational categories of professional, traditional, and uniformed spend more than nonemployed wives (DeWeese and Norton 1991).

Wives' employment also affects clothing expenditures for other family members. An early study (Hafstrom and Dunsing 1965) found that wives' clothing expenditures did not differ between employed and nonemployed wives, but were higher for husbands and children in dual-earner families. Dual-earner couples tend to decrease their own clothing expenditures in favor of their children's (Waldrop 1989). Interestingly, wife's employment in a blue-collar occupation affects clothing expenditures for boys (Nelson 1989), and her employment in a more traditional female occupation positively affects clothing expenditure for girls (DeWeese and Norton 1991).

Total Expenditures

Few studies have surveyed differences in total expenditures by wife's work status. Some household studies examine only aggregate categories and fail to distinguish differentials in disaggregated areas, such as child care or wife's clothing. Most analyses use the Consumer Expenditure Survey, which divides expenditures into fifteen commodity groups, with detailed data in the Detailed Expenditure File (MTAB). The three studies described next use 1972–1973 CE data to compare expenditure patterns of one-earner and dual-earner families.

To determine real-income equivalence between one-earner and two-earner households, Lazear and Michael (1980) transformed the bundle of service flows consumed by the family into market values. They found about a 17 percent difference in total consumption, with two-earner families having relatively large increases for durables, clothing, and transportation, and relatively small increases for services, rental housing, and nondurables. They attributed much of the increased household expenditure, especially on clothing, durables, and transportation, to wife's employment. However, as the studies reviewed above indicate, the spending impact (except transportation) is attributable to the increased income from wife's employment rather than to increased work-related spending.

Vickery (1979) examined income and expenditures of families with employed and nonemployed wives. Over 70 percent of the increased expenditures of working-wife families went to transportation and retirement funds, with decreased spending for shelter. These work-related expenses required about 14 percent of wives' before-tax earnings, and increased taxes were 20 percent. Vickery's most path-breaking conclusion was that goods and services purchased with wives' earnings were similar to those of one-earner families, and were not market substitutes for housework activities.

The impact of demographic factors and wife's employment on the pattern of married-couple expenditures was studied by Ketkar and Cho (1982). Using the full-time or part-time status of both spouses as regression explanatory variables, they found that full-time employment of both positively influenced expenditures on transportation, food-away-from-home, clothing, tobacco, and personal care, and negatively affected expenditures on shelter and recreation. There were significant expenditure differences on work-related categories when the wife worked, and shelter was of lesser importance when both spouses worked, reinforcing Vickery's findings. This conclusion has probably not persisted, given the substantial inflation in housing in the 1970s and early 1980s, when numerous wives entered the labor force to facilitate the purchase of new or larger housing.

Using an institutional economics approach, Brown (1987) developed detailed historical (1918–1980) analyses of the impacts of economic growth on expenditure patterns of families by class and race. She concluded that the shift from basic expenditures (food, clothing, and household operation) to newer consumption bundles reflected increased emphasis on amenities, recreation, transportation, and income security. These new expenditure patterns revealed the families' attempts to maintain their class position and were dominant factors in promoting wives' entry into the labor force.

Analyzing expenditure differences for 1986–1987 between one- and two-earner families, Waldrop (1989) emphasized that most couples are home owners. Dual-earners spend more on household operations, and those with children sacrifice household furnishings to pay for child care. Couples' second highest expenditure is transportation, with dual-earners spending almost a fourth more on transportation than single-earner families. Employed mothers spend 20 percent more on food-away-from-home than one-earner families, but dual-earner childless couples spend 50 percent more on food-away-from-home. Overall, Waldrop finds distinct lifestyle differences between one- and two-earner families, and these contrasts are exacerbated by the presence or absence of children. We conclude that numerous dual-earner childless couples may be "empty nesters," and these lifestyle differences seen in expenditure patterns may be related to their stage in the life cycle.

Studying household consumption patterns, Yang and Magrabi (1989) found that working-wife families allocated larger budget shares to food-away-from-home and private transportation, which is consistent with all the other analyses. These families spent smaller shares on food-at-home, housing, apparel, public transportation, health care, tobacco, and personal insurance. When household characteristics (particularly income level) are controlled, working-wife families spend a larger share only on private transportation. This is consistent with the other findings described above: that wife's contribution to marginal household income is a crucial factor affecting consumption patterns.

Overall, these studies show that many of the perceived differences between the spending patterns of one-earner and dual-earner families relate to income level rather than to wife's work status. Although these studies provide insight on selected expenditures of two-earner families, the results are conflicting. Some of the differences in findings are attributable to the use of different data bases, time periods, and methodologies, and to the selection of independent variables. Most researchers have found significant differences only in expenditures for child care and transportation between one- and two-earner families. In the following sections we report two of our empirical studies that extend previous comparisons between one- and two-earner married-couple families.

COSTS OF WIVES' EMPLOYMENT:
EMPIRICAL STUDY I

This section presents an empirical study of wives' work-related expenses by comparing differences in mean expenditures for selected goods and services between one- and two-earner families. Selected expenditure categories representing the explicit costs of wife's employment are compared by family income level and by the age and number of children. The expenditure differences give a measure of the cost of wife's employment.

The data from the 1986 Consumer Expenditure Survey are limited to married-couple families under age sixty-five, either with or without children. Only complete income reporters[1] and full-time (thirty-five hours or more per week), full-year (fifty weeks) labor force participants are included. Families below the poverty level (income less than $10,000) were excluded to minimize the effects of in-kind transfers. Married-couple families with nonemployed wives (NWW) (N = 744) and full-time working wives (FWW) (N = 2,282) are compared by six net after-tax income levels, with six subgroups by number and age of children.

The selected expenditure categories expected to be higher when wife is in the labor force are (1) child care (both baby-sitting and day care); (2) services (yard care, housekeeping, nonclothing laundry and dry cleaning, and apparel dry cleaning); (3) women's day-wear clothing; (4) food-at-home; (5) food-away-from-home; (6) vehicle purchases; (7) private transportation (operation); and (8) public transportation.

The mean expenditure data for the thirty-six cases (six income classes by six family groups) were analyzed by t-tests for differences in the paired group means. The differenced data clearly indicate that child care is the most important expenditure differential, at all income levels, between single- and dual-earner families with children under six years old. There are very few significant differences between FWW and NWW families at the same level of income on services, clothing, food-at-home and food-away-from-home, and vehicles. Expenditure differences on private transportation are not significant for families with fewer than two children, but are significantly higher for almost 30 percent of FWW families with two children. The data are mixed for public transportation, perhaps because of greater use of public transportation among lower-income families. These findings support the earlier research findings outlined above, and are extended by a more detailed study in the following section.

EXPENDITURE PATTERN DIFFERENTIALS[2]: EMPIRICAL STUDY II

The effects of wives' employment on family expenditure patterns are compared over time with 1972–1973 and 1984 data, distinguishing nonemployed (NWW), full-time (FWW), and part-time employed wives (PWW). The two objectives of this study are to analyze the effects of income, wife's work status, and other selected demographic variables on family expenditure shares; and to examine change in household expenditure patterns over time.

Data and Methodology

Expenditure data are from the Bureau of Labor Statistics Consumer Expenditure Survey (CE) interviews for 1972–1973 and 1984. The data files are limited to complete income reporters, in order to increase accuracy of the net-after-tax regressor. The sample includes only married-couple families under age sixty-five, in which the husband worked full-time, and only nuclear families, that is, no other persons reside with the family (N = 13,394, with 7,550 in 1972–1973 and 5,944 in 1984). In the 1972–1973 data file, 38 percent of families have FWWs, compared with 48 percent in 1984; 18 percent have PWWs, compared with 24 percent in 1984; and 44 percent have NWWs, compared with 28 percent in the 1984 file.

The independent variables are net after-tax income and the demographic variables of family size, age, and region. For 1984 the income categories are less than $20,000; $20,000 to $40,000; $40,000 to $60,000; and $60,000 and above. Comparable constant-dollar income categories were constructed for 1972–1973.[3]

For each of the sixteen expenditure shares, regressions were performed for the three family types (NWW, PWW, FWW). The two regression models are detailed in the appendix to this chapter. We used ordinary least squares to determine the impact of the independent variables on household expenditure shares for each of the two models for 1972–1973 and for 1984. The effect of income is tested in model A, and the effect of wife's work status is tested in model B. Joint F-tests were performed on each group of the demographic variables to determine whether *as a group* they influenced expenditure patterns.

Findings

Table 6.1 shows expenditure shares for the categories, analyzed by wife's work status and family income level for 1972–1973 and 1984. Table 6.2 shows total expenditures and the sample distribution, by wife's work status and family income category, for both time periods. The items reported cover approximately 95 percent of all household expenditures (Gieseman 1987), aggregated into sixteen categories[4] representing major household expenditure areas.[5]

Overall, our findings indicate that expenditure patterns have a fairly high degree of consistency between types of families and income levels, and over time. However, there are some discernible differences, particularly in housing categories and private transportation. The share of total expenditures for food-at-home displays remarkable consistency between household types and over time. As expected, these expenditure shares decrease as income increases. Expenditure shares on food-away-from-home remained constant between household types over time, except for income levels over $60,000, for which expenditure shares were 2–3 percent higher in 1984 for all three household types. Expenditures on alcohol and tobacco did not vary by more than 1 percent between any two categories.

Most families had a 2–6 percent higher expenditure share on owned dwellings in 1984 than in 1972–1973. The sole exception was FWW families with incomes less than $20,000. For rented dwellings, families allocated a 1–2 percent larger expenditure share in 1984 than previously, except higher-income NWW families. For household operations, expen-

Table 6.1

Expenditure Shares (percent) by Wife's Work Status and Income Category, 1972–1973 and 1984

| | | Wife's Work Status | | | | | |
| | | Non-Working | | Part-Time | | Full-Time | |
	Income Category	1972 -1973	1984	1972 -1973	1984	1972 -1973	1984
Food-at-Home	<$20,000	15	14	17	16	17	17
	$20-40,000	13	13	13	13	14	15
	$40-60,000	11	11	13	11	11	11
	>$60,000	12	10	10	12	12	10
Food-Away	<$20,000	4	4	4	4	4	4
	$20-40,000	5	5	4	5	4	4
	$40-60,000	5	6	5	5	5	5
	>$60,000	4	7	4	6	5	7
Alcohol & Tobacco	<$20,000	3	3	3	3	3	3
	$20-40,000	2	3	2	2	2	2
	$40-60,000	3	2	2	2	2	2
	>$60,000	2	2	3	2	2	2
Owned Dwelling	<$20,000	7	9	9	11	9	9
	$20-40,000	10	12	12	15	13	16
	$40-60,000	11	17	13	19	15	17
	>$60,000	12	18	11	16	14	16
Rented Dwelling	<$20,000	9	10	7	9	8	9
	$20-40,000	5	6	4	5	3	4
	$40-60,000	3	3	0	2	2	3
	>$60,000	4	3	2	4	1	3
Household Oper.	<$20,000	8	11	8	10	8	12
	$20-40,000	8	11	8	11	8	11
	$40-60,000	9	10	8	10	9	11
	>$60,000	9	11	10	12	9	11
Furnish. & Equip.	<$20,000	5	4	5	4	5	5
	$20-40,000	6	4	6	5	6	5
	$40-60,000	6	5	5	5	8	7
	>$60,000	5	7	6	6	6	5
Apparel & Service	<$20,000	9	6	8	6	8	5
	$20-40,000	9	6	9	6	9	5
	$40-60,000	11	7	9	7	10	9
	>$60,000	8	10	12	8	12	8

Table 6.1 (continued)

| | | Wife's Work Status | | | | | |
| | | Non-Working | | Part-Time | | Full-Time | |
	Income Category	1972 -1973	1984	1972 -1973	1984	1972 -1973	1984
Private Trans	<$20,000	23	25	21	19	21	18
	$20-40,000	22	24	19	21	20	19
	$40-60,000	15	22	19	19	15	17
	>$60,000	20	14	15	17	15	14
Public Trans	<$20,000	1	1	1	1	1	1
	$20-40,000	1	1	1	1	1	1
	$40-60,000	3	2	1	2	2	2
	>$60,000	1	4	3	2	2	2
Health Care	<$20,000	5	4	5	4	5	5
	$20-40,000	4	4	5	4	5	4
	$40-60,000	3	2	1	2	2	2
	>$60,000	5	3	6	3	3	3
Entertainment	<$20,000	5	5	4	6	5	5
	$20-40,000	5	6	7	6	6	7
	$40-60,000	6	7	6	6	5	8
	>$60,000	6	7	6	7	6	10
Personal Care	<$20,000	1	1	1	1	1	1
	$20-40,000	1	1	1	1	1	1
	$40-60,000	1	1	1	1	1	1
	>$60,000	1	1	1	1	1	1
Reading & Educ.	<$20,000	1	2	1	3	1	3
	$20-40,000	2	2	3	2	2	2
	$40-60,000	5	2	6	3	3	2
	>$60,000	5	2	4	2	4	3
Miscellaneous	<$20,000	1	1	1	1	1	1
	$20-40,000	1	1	1	1	1	1
	$40-60,000	0	1	0	1	1	1
	>$60,000	0	1	0	1	0	1
Life Insurance	<$20,000	4	2	4	2	4	1
	$20-40,000	6	2	6	2	5	2
	$40-60,000	7	2	7	4	7	1
	>$60,000	6	2	7	2	7	3

Source: R. M. Rubin, B. J. Riney, and D. J. Molina (1990). Expenditure Pattern Differentials Between One-Earner and Dual-Earner Households: 1972–1973 and 1984. *Journal of Consumer Research* 17(1), 43–53. © 1990 by Journal of Consumer Research, Inc. All rights reserved.

Table 6.2
Total Family Expenditures by Income Category (nominal dollars) and Sample Distribution,
1972–1973 and 1984

	Wife's Work Status					
	Non-Working		Part-Time Work		Full-Time Work	
Expenditures	1972-1973	1984	1972-1973	1984	1972-1973	1984
Total Expenditure						
<$20,000	$12,789,966	$13,096,763	$7,172,454	$7,795,840	$18,393,490	$11,349,685
$20-40,000	16,514,645	33,927,617	6,542,947	16,354,738	13,258,166	14,670,969
$40-60,000	1,433,458	16,130,232	551,695	6,034,828	2,126,028	5,783,633
>$60,000	503,952	7,780,582	422,988	3,869,301	1,216,219	4,536,381
Total per Household	11,008	25,092	10,731	23,421	10,468	21,852
Sample Distribution						
<$20,000	1,460	684	839	467	2,209	728
$20-40,000	1,276	1,442	488	732	970	666
$40-60,000	78	505	27	178	113	172
>$60,000	24	196	15	77	51	97

Source: R. M. Rubin, B. J. Riney, and D. J. Molina (1990). Expenditure Pattern Differentials Between One-Earner and Dual-Earner Households: 1972–1973 and 1984. *Journal of Consumer Research* 17(1), 43–53. © by Journal of Consumer Research, Inc. All rights reserved.

diture shares were consistently 2–4 percent higher for all income categories in 1984 than in 1972–1973. In contrast, the expenditure share of housefurnishings and equipment decreased or remained constant from 1972–1973 to 1984, except for NWW families with incomes over $60,000. A similar pattern held for apparel and services, but the decline was even more pronounced.

Expenditure shares for private transportation reveal quite different and unexpected patterns of change over time. These shares declined for FWW families and increased for NWW families over time, while the pattern for PWW families was mixed. Public transportation shares increased with income in both periods.

The share for the smaller expenditure categories (health care, reading and education, and life and personal insurance) decreased from 1972–1973 to 1984 for all household types and income levels, with one exception. This is the increase for reading and education for all family types under $20,000 income level. Entertainment shares increased slightly or remained constant over time for the three household types, except for high-income FWW families, which showed a substantial increase in 1984.

Between the two time periods, shares increased for owned dwelling, rented dwelling, household operations, and entertainment. Shares decreased for housefurnishings and equipment, apparel and services, health care, reading and education, and life and personal insurance. Those for food-at-home and away, alcohol and tobacco, public transportation, and personal care changed little. The most anomalous household category is the high-income, husband-only-earner, which is the exception to several of the general expenditure patterns.

To study expenditure differentials further, F-tests were applied to four demographic variables (income level, region, family size, wife's age), in addition to the overall F-test for the model. Household expenditures shares analyzed by wife's work status are shown in Table 6.3. The individual group F-tests and the model F-tests do not reveal clearly defined patterns of the demographic variables. This result reaffirms the findings for durables by Strober (1977) and Strober and Weinberg (1977).

For 1972–1973, income was a significant determinant of most expenditures for FWW families, and for about half the expenditure categories for the other two family types. For 1984, income was a more similar determinant of expenditures for the NWW and FWW than for PWW families. This may reflect household perceptions that part-time income is transitory rather than permanent (Friedman 1957), an important finding. Our findings are generally consistent with those of Lazear and Michael (1988) for FWWs. They found that while the employment status of both

Table 6.3
Impact of Income Level and Demographic Variables on Expenditure Shares by Wife's Work Status, 1972–1973 and 1984

| | Wife's Work Status | | | | | |
| | Non-Working | | Part-Time | | Full-Time | |
Expenditure Category	1972–1973	1984	1972–1973	1984	1972–1973	1984
Food-at-Home	ISA+	ISA+	ISA+	IS+	ISA+	IS+
Food-Away	-	IA+	-	S+	I	ISA+
Alcohol & Tobacco	R	ISAR+	S+	ISR+	IS+	I
Owned Dwelling	I+	I+	IA+	IS+	IA+	I+
Rented Dwelling	ISAR	IA+	ISA+	ISA+	ISAR+	IAR+
Household Oper.	-	SAR+	R+	R+	IR+	R+
Furnish. & Equip.	SA+	IS+	A	-	IA+	+
Apparel & Service	I+	I+	I	A	I+	I+
Private Trans.	I+	I+	I	A	IA+	
Public Trans.	ISR+	I+	IS+	S+	ISR+	I+
Health Care	-	A+	-	I+	I+	I+
Entertainment	AR+	I+	-	-	-	I+
Personal Care	A+	SA+	A+	-	A+	S
Reading & Educ.	ISA+	A+	IA+	A	ISA+	-
Miscellaneous	IAR+	-	IAR+	-	IS+	-
Life Insurance	I+	A+	I	-	ISAR+	I+

Note: I = income level, R = region, S = family size, A = age of wife, + = significant F-test for the model.

Source: R. M. Rubin, B. J. Riney, and D. J. Molina (1990). Expenditure Pattern Differentials Between One-Earner and Dual-Earner Households: 1972–1973 and 1984. *Journal of Consumer Research* 17(1), 43–53. © by Journal of Consumer Research, Inc. All rights reserved.

spouses affects the pattern of household spending, wife's part-time employment had a larger impact than her full-time employment, which we did not find.

In 1972–1973, family size was a greater determinant of expenditures for the FWW household than for the NWW and PWW families. The opposite was true in 1984. In all cases family size affected food-at-home, and in most cases it affected rented dwellings, alcohol and tobacco, and public transportation. The impact of wife's age on household expenditure shares was consistent over all three types of families in 1972–1973, but in 1984 it varied across household types. The impact of age was considerably greater for NWW than for working-wife families in 1984. For PWWs, age was significant for expenditures on rented dwellings, apparel, private transportation, and reading and education; for FWWs, age was significant only for food-away-from-home and rented dwellings. As with family size,

Table 6.4

Impact of Demographic Variables on Expenditure Shares by Family Income Level, 1972–1973 and 1984

Expenditure Category	<$20,000 1972–1973	<$20,000 1984	$20–40,000 1972–1973	$20–40,000 1984	$40–60,000 1972–1973	$40–60,000 1984	>$60,000 1972–1973	>$60,000 1984
Food-at-Home	RSAW+	SW+	SA+	SAW+	S+	S+	-	-
Food-Away	W	SA+	+	AW+	-	A+	-	S+
Alcohol, Tobacco	RS+	R	S	RS+	-	R+	-	-
Owned Dwelling	RSAW+	A	AW+	A	-	S	A+	-
Rented Dwelling	RSA+	A+	RSA+	RAW+	-	SA+	RS+	A
Household Oper.	RS+	R+	RSA+	R	-	RS	-	-
Housefur., Equip.	SA+	S	A+	-	A+	-	-	-
Apparel, Service	RSW+	-	-	A+	-	R	-	-
Private Trans.	RSW+	SW+	AW+	-	A	-	-	-
Public Trans.	RS+	A	RSA+	RA+	RS+	S	R	-
Health Care	RSA+	-	RW+	RA+	-	A	-	-
Entertainment	RA+	A+	-	-	-	-	-	A
Personal Care	RAW+	A+	SA+	-	A+	-	-	-
Reading, Educ.	A+	-	RSA+	A+	SA+	A+	SA+	A+
Miscellaneous	RAW+	-	R+	-	S	-	-	-
Life Insurance	RA+	A	RS	RA+	-	-	A	A

Note: R = region, S = family size, A = age of wife, W = work status of wife, + = significant F-test for the model.

Source: R. M. Rubin, B. J. Riney, and D. J. Molina (1990). Expenditure Pattern Differentials Between One-Earner and Dual-Earner Households: 1972–1973 and 1984. *Journal of Consumer Research* 17(1), 43–53. © by Journal of Consumer Research, Inc. All rights reserved.

age of wife is significant in all categories for rented dwellings in both periods. Region is not a significant determinant of expenditure share when analyzed by wife's work status. Finally, the performance of the equations (as tested by the model F-test) does not provide a clear pattern, but income and the other demographic variables cannot be excluded as a total group.

Analyzing expenditure patterns by household income level (Table 6.4), we find for both 1972–1973 and 1984 that the demographic variables (either as individual groups or as a whole) have a greater impact on expenditure shares at the two lower income levels than at the two higher levels. Wife's work status is significant for only a few expenditure categories, and then only for the two lower income levels. In 1972–1973, wife's employment status is significant for seven expenditure categories at incomes under $20,000; it is significant for only three expenditure categories at income level $20,000–40,000; and it is not a significant determinant of expenditure at higher income levels. In contrast, in 1984 the impact of wife's work status is significant for three expenditure categories at the $20,000–40,000 income level and for two expenditure categories for income level under $20,000. Thus, the importance of wife's work status to household expenditures declined over time, even at lower income. This important finding indicates that family expenditure patterns are converging, regardless of wife' work status, and this convergence is more notable at income below $20,000.

For income under $20,000 in 1972–1973, region was a significant determinant of all expenditures except food-away-from-home, housefurnishings and equipment, and reading and education. For higher income levels in 1972–1973 and for all income levels in 1984, region of residence was a much less significant explanatory variable, except in the expected categories of utilities, rent, and public transportation.

In 1972–1973 the coefficient of family size was significant for most major expenditure categories for income levels less than $40,000; it was much less important in 1984. For incomes over $60,000, family size was not a significant determinant of expenditure shares. Age of wife is a significant determinant of expenditure shares. For both 1972–1973 and 1984, the coefficient of age is significant for about half of all expenditure categories when household income is less than $40,000, and for one-quarter of expenditure shares for incomes over $40,000.

Conclusions

The central question addressed in this study is, Do one-earner and two types of dual-earner families at the same level of after-tax income allocate income among major expenditure categories differently, and does this pattern change over time? This extensive cross-sectional analysis of household expenditure shares indicates that expenditure patterns have a fairly high degree of consistency between types of families in terms of wife's work status and income levels, and over time. The major expenditure differences over time are increases in the shares for housing and household operation and decreases in the shares for health care, reading and education, and life and personal insurance. These findings may reflect the impacts of two different economic trends: housing inflation combined with mortgage rate increases and increases in fringe benefits during the period studied. Further, expenditure shares on private transportation increased for NWW families and declined for PWW and FWW households. This finding may reflect a trade-off with the somewhat larger expenditure share of owned dwelling and household operations of working-wife families.

The finding that income is a more similar determinant of expenditures for NWW and FWW than for PWW families in 1984 may reflect household perceptions that part-time income is transitory (Friedman 1957). Wife's work status was more important in 1972–1973 than in 1984 at the lowest income level; it had about the same degree of impact at the $20,000 to $40,000 income level in both periods. The findings indicate greater impact of other demographic variables on expenditure shares at the two lower income levels than at the two higher income levels, for both 1972–1973 and 1984.

In addition, we analyzed the effects of a series of demographic variables on expenditure shares for the different types of families and different income levels. When analyzed by wife's work status, income is the most important determinant of household expenditures. Income was significant for twice as many expenditure categories for NWW and FWW as for PWW families. In 1984, the impact of family size and age on expenditures decreased for FWW families, compared with the other two family types, which was not the case in 1972–1973. This may reflect the increased labor force commitment of wives in 1984.

When analyzed by household income level, demographic variables are in general less significant for families with income levels over $40,000 in both 1972–1973 and 1984. In particular, wife's work status was an important determinant of expenditures only for families with income less than $40,000. While the impact of wife's age on expenditures is as important in 1984 as in 1972–1973, region and family size are less important over time.

APPENDIX

In the second empirical study presented in this chapter, expenditure shares are analyzed as a function of net income and the series of demographic variables outlined in the text. The general form of the model is

$$E = f(Y, S, A, R, NWW, FWW, PWW),$$

where

E	=	expenditure share
Y	=	household net income
S	=	family size
A	=	wife's age
R	=	geographic region
NWW	=	household with nonworking wife

PWW = household with part-time working wife (< 35 hours per week)

FWW = household with full-time working wife (= or > 35 hours per week).

The dependent variables are the average expenditure shares on the sixteen expenditure groups for each possible cell for each variable group. Each average expenditure share calculated is the group mean expenditure as a percent of total expenditures of that group for each category. The independent variables for each cell are represented by the demographic dummy variables of net income level, family size, age of wife, geographic region, and wife's work status.[6]

To analyze the expenditure patterns, the average expenditure share for each cell was constructed. The cells were constituted by all of the possible combinations of the demographic variables outlined above. For instance, the first cell for 1984 would be those families where the wife did not work, household income was below $20,000, there were no children, wife's age was under thirty-five, and they resided in the North. Following this procedure, there were 384 possible cells. After deleting characteristic cells with zero observations, we had 304 cells for 1972–1973 and 352 for 1984.

To analyze the impact that family income, wife's work status, and the demographic variables had on family expenditure patterns, we used two separate models for each of the two periods. In model A, the expenditure patterns were analyzed by holding wife's work status constant. For each of the sixteen expenditure shares three regressions were performed, depending on whether the families belonged to NWW, PWW, or FWW. In model B the expenditure patterns were analyzed by holding household income level constant for each income class. Four income classes were used, with 1972–1973 incomes adjusted for inflation to a 1984 constant-dollar level.

MODEL A—by family size

$$E_i = a + b_1 Y_1 + b_2 Y_2 + b_3 Y_3 + b_5 S_1 + b_6 S_2 + b_7 S_3 + b_9 A + b_{11} RN + b_{12} RM + b_{13} RS + u$$

MODEL B—by wife's work status

$$E_i = a + b_5 S_1 + b_6 S_2 + b_7 S_3 + b_9 A_1 + b_{11} RN + b_{12} RM + b_{13} RS + b_{15} NWW + b_{16} PWW + u,$$

where

E_i = expenditure share, i = 1–16

Y_1 = 1 if less than \$20,000 for 1984; 1 if less than \$14,184 for 1972–1973; 0 otherwise

Y_2 = 1 if \$20,000 to \$40,000 for 1984; 1 if \$14,184 to \$28,369 for 1972–1973; 0 otherwise

Y_3 = 1 if \$40,000 to \$60,000 for 1984; 1 if \$28,369 to \$42,553 for 1972–1973; 0 otherwise

Y_4 = 1 if over \$60,000 for 1984; 1 if over \$42,553 for 1972–1973; 0 otherwise

S_1 = 1 if husband-wife with no children; 0 otherwise

S_2 = 1 if husband-wife with one child; 0 otherwise

S_3 = 1 if husband-wife with two children; 0 otherwise

S_4 = 1 if husband-wife with more than two children; 0 otherwise

A_1 = 1 if wife's age less than or equal to 35; 0 otherwise

A_2 = 1 if wife's age greater than 35; 0 otherwise

RN = 1 if North; 0 otherwise

RM = 1 if Midwest (termed Northcentral in 1972–1973 CE); 0 otherwise

RS = 1 if South; 0 otherwise

RW = 1 if West; 0 otherwise

u = error term.

Ordinary least squares was applied to determine the impact of each of the independent variables on household expenditure shares for each of the two models in each period. Joint F-tests were then performed on each group of the demographic variables to determine whether *as a group* they influenced expenditure patterns. Thus, for 1972–1973 and for 1984, family size, age, and region were tested for each of the models. In addition, model A tested the effect of income and model B tested wife's work status. A .05 level of significance determined the impact of the demographic and income variables on expenditure patterns.

Household expenditure share is specified as a linear function of net income for model A (or wife's work status for model B) and a series of relevant demographic variables: family size, wife's age, and geographic region. Family size is included in the model because it affects household expenditures (Foster et al. 1981; Ketkar and Cho 1982; Jacobs et al. 1988), and therefore expenditure share patterns. Family sizes of two (husband and wife with no children), three (husband and wife with one child), four (husband and wife with two children), and five or more (husband and wife with more than two children) are used. We aggregated households with more than two children because of the limited number of larger families in the CE sample.

While some studies use age of reference person (Jacobs et al. 1988; Ketkar and Cho 1982) or husband's age (Foster et al. 1981; Strober and Weinberg 1977), we use wife's age as an indicator of life-cycle stage. Wife's age of less than or equal to thirty-five is viewed as indicative of the childbearing and family formation period. We use the four CE geographic regions of North, Midwest (termed Northcentral in the 1972–1973 CE), South, and West.

Wife's work status is the major focus of our concern. It is defined as (1) the wife is not employed outside the home (NWW), (2) the wife works full-time, thirty-five hours or more per week (FWW), or the wife works part-time, less than thirty-five hours per week (PWW). This breakdown, used in a few studies (Jacobs et al. 1988; Ketkar and Cho 1982), is based on the thirty-five-hour minimum standard workweek in the United States (Hamermesh and Rees 1988) and employs the definitions of full-time and part-time found in the CE documentation (U.S. Department of Labor, Bureau of Labor Statistics, 1979, 1986).

NOTES

1. As defined by the Bureau of Labor Statistics, complete income reporters are "In general, a consumer unit who provided values for at least one of the major sources of its income, such as wages and salaries, self-employment income, and Social Security income. Even complete income reporters may not have provided a full accounting of all income from all sources" (U.S. Department of Labor 1987b; Jacobs et al. 1988).

2. This study appeared in R. M. Rubin, B. J. Riney, and D. J. Molina, Expenditure pattern differentials between one-earner and dual-earner households: 1972–1973 and 1984, *Journal of Consumer Research* 17(1) (1990): 43–53. The authors wish to recognize the contribution of Dr. David Molina, associate professor of economics, University of North Texas, to this research.

3. For 1972–1973 data, the 1984 income categories were deflated to the 1972 level, using the Consumer Price Index (CPI) to make adjusted 1972 income levels of comparable purchasing power. The 1972–1973 income categories are less than $14,184; $14,184 to $28,369; $28,369 to $42,553; and over $42,553. Since these 1972–1973 income categories were made comparable in purchasing power to the 1984 income levels, all references to income levels are in the 1984 amounts.

4. This aggregation was done by grouping CE expenditure codings for 1972–1973 and 1984, following the concordance developed by the Bureau of Labor Statistics (U.S. Department of Labor 1981).

5. Use of education and race as additional independent variables was attempted. Education was not available for 1972–1973, and since it was desirable to include 1972–1973 data to expand the sample base, education was not included. In analyzing the impact of race, the number of black households meeting our sample criteria at upper income levels in 1972–1973 made sample sizes of these cells too small for analysis.

6. By using the mean of each cell, the average representative household's expenditure per cell is analyzed without the problem of having many zeros as independent variables. Since the thrust of this analysis is to determine whether the demographic and income variables impact the expenditure shares of the representative households, and not to predict the amount spent on each share, we use a linear expenditure share approach rather than a multiplicative choice model (Cooper and Nakanishi 1983; Nakanishi and Cooper 1974).

7

Impact of Wife's Employment on Family Income and Assets

Following over a quarter-century of unprecedented economic growth, two important and interrelated economic trends occurred during the period 1973–1986: the continuing dramatic rise in women's labor force participation and the general stagnation of wages in the United States. This chapter explores the income effects of the concurrence of these two major trends, with an analysis of income and asset differentials between one-earner and dual-earner families for 1972–1973 and 1986. The next two sections present a brief perspective on the economic background for this period and a review of studies of the relationships between wives' earnings and family income and wealth. The last section is our empirical analysis of the impacts of wife's employment status on family income and assets between 1972–1973 and 1986.

ECONOMIC BACKGROUND

The years from the end of World War II to 1973 were an extended period of wage and real income growth, based primarily on productivity increases and innovations in products and production (Litan et al. 1988). Following this expansionary period, there was a notable shift in the growth of real income. From 1973 to at least 1986, inflation-adjusted wages stagnated (Levy 1988a). Average household income would have grown even less, in constant dollars, if the increasing prevalence of two-earner families had not occurred (Litan et al. 1988). After rising for nearly three decades, men's real earnings (adjusted for inflation) were virtually flat during the 1970s.

The real income of families with one male earner declined. Doubtless, many wives entered the labor market or increased their participation to improve or maintain their household standard of living.

The increased number of employed wives has changed family incomes, as wives' employment status has positively affected the financial resources of dual-earner families relative to one-earner and to all other households. In 1970, median income for husband-as-sole-earner families was $9,304, compared with $12,276 for dual-earner families, a difference of 32 percent. In 1986, this difference had increased to 49 percent, with dual-earner median income of $38,346, one-earner married-couple median income of $25,803, and all families' median income of $29,458 (U.S. Bureau of the Census 1991).

A paradox of this 1973–1986 period was that while earnings per worker stagnated, income per capita increased from $9,926 in 1973 (in 1987 dollars) to $12,150 in 1987 (Levy 1988b). Levy (1988b) explained this apparent contradiction as primarily due to the growth of two-paycheck families and, secondarily, to smaller families, which is related to wives' increased labor force participation.

WIVES' EARNINGS

Previous researchers have examined the effects of wives' employment status and earnings on household income and wealth. Although for many years wives' earnings constituted about one-fourth of family income, Bell (1976), in a seminal study, cautioned that viewing wives' contribution from this overall perspective is a misleading oversimplification. She emphasized that wives' earnings are more meaningful in studies using disaggregated analyses. She used 1972 data from the Current Population Reports to analyze earnings of working wives by occupation, part-time and full-time employment status, age, and husband's earnings to illustrate the impacts of their economic contribution to different households. In particular, disaggregation reveals the importance of wife's earnings contribution to the total income of lower-income families. Since Bell's research, wives' earnings have become even more important and for a much wider range of family income levels.

Between 1969 and 1985, average inflation-adjusted income of dual-earner families increased 17 percent for white households and 38 percent for black, in contrast to only 7 percent and 5.5 percent, respectively, for one-earner married-couple families. In an analysis of employed wives' share of family income from Current Population Survey data, the percent of income contributed by wife's earnings increased from 28 percent in

1969 to 30 percent in 1985. Dual-earner families in 1985 were almost twice as likely as households in general to be in the top income quintile (Blank 1988).

A study (Avery and Elliehausen 1986) using the 1983 Survey of Consumer Finances data to analyze high-income families (defined as those with incomes over $50,000) found that 56 percent in the $50,000–99,999 income group were dual-earner. However, the share of dual-earner families declined as income increased, with 39 percent, 38 percent, and 31 percent, respectively, in the $100,000–149,999, $150,000–279,999, and $280,000 or more categories. A Brookings Institution study (Levy 1988b) concluded that the share of families with incomes over $50,000 has increased, primarily due to the increasing number of dual-earner families. A fourth of dual-earner families had incomes over $50,000 (in constant 1987 dollars) in both 1973 and 1986, and with the growth of dual-earner families, the share of the income distribution at that level increased correspondingly. By 1990, wife's paycheck was needed to promote three-fifths of these higher-income families into the $50,000 and over income category (Linden 1990).

Several studies have extended the concept of real income to encompass the total of money, or nominal, income plus the value of home-produced goods and services. Recognizing the increase in nominal household income, Michael (1985) looked at the gain in the total of earned and home-production income from wife's employment. His findings are consistent with the earlier analysis of Lazear and Michael (1980), and suggest that the effect on total income is considerably smaller than the effect on nominal income.

Earned income from wages and salaries constitutes almost 90 percent of all family income for nonelderly married couples; only 5 percent is from public or private transfers (Blank 1988), with the remainder being asset income. Although most household income derives from earned income,[1] wealth holdings and income from wealth influence household financial well-being. Wealth determines consumer savings, consumption, and other financial behavior, and generates current income and access to credit and mortgage debt.

In developing the permanent income hypothesis, Friedman (1957) assumed that wife's income was transitory and that a greater marginal propensity to save was attached to it than to income from other sources. Married women's labor force attachment is more permanent now than when this theory was postulated, so we assume the effect of wives' earnings on family asset accumulation has changed.

There is growing evidence of a declining propensity to save relative to disposable income for all households. In an extensive analysis of household asset holdings from the 1983 Survey of Consumer Finances, substantial reductions were found in the proportion of families with savings accounts, bonds, and stocks since 1977 (Avery et al. 1984a, 1984b). Another analysis reported a slowdown in the growth of household wealth in the 1969–1983 period, overlapping the period under study, and the biggest relative growth among financial assets in deposits in financial institutions (Wolff 1989).

A study of wife's earnings and family wealth, using 1972–1973 CE data, concluded that households with full-time employed wives had lower levels of wealth, financial assets, and home equity than families of full-time homemakers. Further, the level of financial assets and total wealth were negatively associated with wife's part-time employment status, but the differences were much narrower than for families with a full-time employed wife (Foster and Rakhshani 1983).

FAMILY INCOME AND ASSETS: EMPIRICAL ANALYSIS

In this section, our empirical analysis expands previous research on the effects of wives' earnings on family income. Distinguishing between families with nonworking (NWW), full-time (FWW), and part-time (PWW) employed wives, we compare family income and asset patterns over time for 1972–1973 and 1986, the crucial period of stagnant wage growth.

We compare the differences in the pre-tax income, after-tax income, and selected financial assets of three types of families, based on wife's employment status. This comparison reveals the differences between one-earner families with a nonemployed wife (NWW) and dual-earner families with a full-time employed wife (FWW) and with a part-time employed wife (PWW). The underlying question is whether wives' income in dual-earner families has, at least in part, compensated for the stagnation in the growth of wages and real income. The objectives were to determine whether wife's employment status and other demographic variables influenced pre-tax and after-tax income and assets of married-couple families, and if so, whether the effect changed between 1972–1973 and 1986.

Data and Methodology

The data base for this study contained three files derived from the 1972–1973 and 1986 Consumer Expenditure (CE) Interview Surveys. We analyzed married-couple families with a full-time employed husband and with the wife employed part-time, full-time, or not at all (and in which there were no other workers). These families were separated into four income categories from $10,000 to $99,999. We analyzed four types of financial assets from the CE data: checking accounts, savings accounts, stocks and bonds, and U.S. government bonds.[2] The data were limited to complete income reporters in urban areas, to nonelderly families, and to home owners with and without mortgages or to renters. Households with incomes below the poverty level of $3,934 in 1972–1973 and $10,000 in 1986 were excluded. Application of these screening criteria produced 6,357 married-couple families for 1972–1973 and 2,388 for 1986.

This study addressed the influence of wife's employment status and the demographic variables of wife's age, family composition, and home ownership on the income and assets of married-couple households. We first analyzed the sample mean income and asset data, then examined regression results, and also applied analysis of variance (ANOVA) for wife's employment status. The second research question concerned whether family income and selected assets changed between 1972–1973 and 1986. We used both regression and ANOVA for this analysis. The methodology and models used are detailed in the chapter appendix.

Findings

Income and Assets. Table 7.1 presents mean income and assets for families with the three types of wife's employment status for 1972–1973 and 1986, in constant 1986 dollars. Most notably, the data reveal that both husband's earnings and other incomes declined for all three family types between 1972–1973 and 1986. For families with full-time employed wives, wife's earnings increased sufficiently to prevent a decline in family pre-tax earnings, but this was not the case for part-time working wives. Wife's earnings increased absolutely and, calculated from the data in Table 7.1, as a share of household income, from 32 percent to 38 percent for full-time, and from 12 percent to 17 percent for part-time.[3] This means that husbands' earnings declined as a share of income in dual-income families.

While gross or pre-tax income gives some measure of households' equity relationship to other households, after-tax or spendable income is

Table 7.1
Mean Income and Assets by Wife's Work Status, 1972–1973 and 1986 (in constant 1986 dollars)

Income and Assets	Wife's Work Status					
	Full-Time		Part-Time		Non-Working	
	1972–1973 (N=2348)	1986 (N=1278)	1972–1973 (N=1186)	1986 (N=510)	1972–1973 (N=2657)	1986 (N=575)
Pretax Income	$43,479	$42,012	$39,727	$36,973	$38,083	$34,407
Total Earnings	40,397	41,162	36,280	36,148	34,531	33,561
By Husband	26,541	25,165	31,433	29,976	34,531	33,561
By Wife	13,856	15,998	4,846	6,171	0	0
Other Incomes	1,311	847	1,349	795	1,415	816
After-tax Income	36,703	37,536	34,256	33,880	32,726	31,169
Total Tax Paid	6,777	4,476	5,470	3,093	5,356	3,238
Assets	13,077	4,321	10,906	5,741	13,967	4,414
Checking Accounts	1,021	669	763	715	952	454
Savings Accounts	6,906	2,323	5,506	2,952	7,305	2,270
Stocks and Bonds	4,136	1,241	4,010	1,938	4,859	1,579
U.S. Bonds	1,013	87	627	136	851	112

Assets by Income Level

$10,000–20,000	2,002	451	1,850	652	2,517	1,022
Checking Accounts	351	135	207	110	252	107
Savings Accounts	1,038	295	1,349	529	2,004	893
Stocks and Bonds	480	0	179	0	169	5
U.S. Bonds	133	21	115	14	92	17
20,000–40,000	4,989	1,535	5,631	3,216	7,969	1,360
Checking Accounts	568	243	580	600	635	295
Savings Accounts	3,380	998	3,560	1,971	4,281	1,537
Stocks and Bonds	746	252	892	599	2,330	420
U.S. Bonds	295	43	599	46	724	109
40,000–60,000	13,222	4,687	14,644	10,003	20,128	7,826
Checking Accounts	1,278	681	880	1,209	1,166	794
Savings Accounts	7,798	2,784	7,378	4,726	11,037	3,448
Stocks and Bonds	2,925	3,784	5,588	3,784	6,893	3,321
U.S. Bonds	1,221	101	797	284	1,033	262
60,000–100,000	37,599	13,422	30,107	14,791	38,116	12,971
Checking Accounts	1,795	2,131	1,645	1,058	2,602	1,134
Savings Accounts	15,994	6,096	11,768	6,877	17,444	5,675
Stocks and Bonds	17,154	4,980	16,061	6,472	16,281	6,118
U.S. Bonds	2,656	214	633	383	1,789	44

Source: Consumer Expenditure Survey interview tapes 1972–1973 and 1986.

Figure 7.1
**Mean Household Assets by Income Level and Wife's Work Status,
1972–1973 and 1986 (in constant 1986 dollars)**

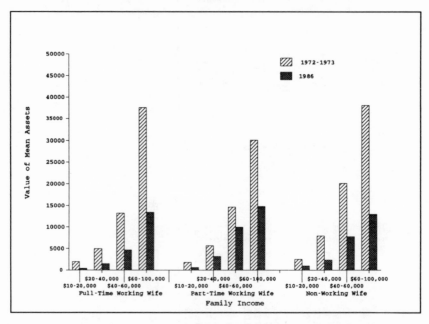

Source: Consumer Expenditure Survey interview tapes 1972–1973 and 1986.

a more accurate measure of the family's access to goods and services. Further, the number of earners affects household taxes and deductions, such as the child care deduction. The mean data show that after-tax income also declined for PWW and NWW families, but increased for FWW families. This may have resulted from the decline in marginal tax rates in the 1980s, which helped dual-earners partially overcome the income effects of stagnation.

Between 1972–1973 and 1986, average assets (in constant 1986 dollars) declined by over two-thirds for FWW and NWW families, and fell by almost one-half for PWW families. There are two probable explanations for this finding. First, since incomes failed to keep pace with inflation, families probably spent a larger share of income on consumption. Second, the high rates of inflation during the study period, especially the early 1980s, may have induced people to invest in commodities or housing rather than financial assets.

Assets (in constant 1986 dollars) for the three types of families are shown in Figure 7.1, by income level and wife's work status for 1972–

Figure 7.2

Mean Household Assets by Family Size and Wife's Work Status, 1972–1973 and 1986 (in constant 1986 dollars)

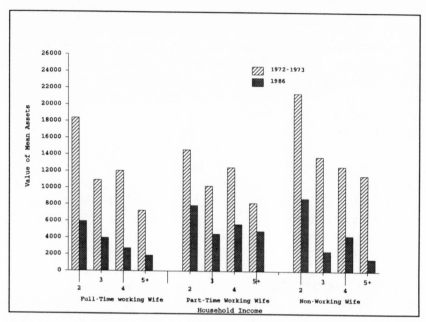

Source: Consumer Expenditure Survey interview tapes 1972–1973 and 1986.

1973 and 1986. The group means presented are averages for all families in the group, including those with zero holdings of the asset, which reduces the average values. The most striking aspect of comparing these two sets of cross-sectional data is the very substantial decline over this period in these assets for the three family groups. This finding is consistent with previous findings that reported reductions in the proportion of families with savings accounts, bonds, and stocks from 1970 to 1983 (Avery et al., 1984a, 1984b).

In 1972–1973, NWW families had the highest asset levels in all income categories. By 1986, PWW families were the largest asset holders, although the amounts had declined. This may substantiate Friedman's (1957) permanent income hypothesis for part-time-employed wives. Assets (in constant 1986 dollars) for the three types of families, by family size and wife's work status, are shown in Figure 7.2 for 1972–1973 and 1986. Mean assets decreased as family size increases for all three household types. The decline was greatest as family composition moved from no children to any number of children in both 1972–1973 and 1986.[4] For families with children, asset holdings consistently declined, both over time and over household type.

Results of Regression Analysis. The impact of four independent variables (wife's employment status, wife's age, family composition, and home ownership) on the dependent variables (pre-tax income, after-tax income, and assets) was analyzed, using regression analysis at the .05 level of significance. The hypothesis was that the independent variables of wife's employment status, wife's age, family composition, and home ownership positively impacted pre-tax income, after-tax income, and financial assets of married-couple families. If an impact was found, the second hypothesis was that the effect is the same for 1972–1973 and 1986.

The results indicate that all four independent variables are significant for both pre-tax and after-tax income. The F-test result for wife's employment status and pre-tax income was 17.83, for wife's age 56.98, for family composition 3.10, and for home ownership 57.07.[5] The F-test result for after-tax income for wife's work status was 16.05, for wife's age 51.07, for family composition 3.92, and for home ownership 59.98.

The regression coefficients for comparison between 1972–1973 and 1986 are shown in Table 7.2. Of the independent variables tested, wife's work status (both FWW and PWW) significantly influenced pre-tax and after-tax income in both periods; but its impact was significantly greater in 1972–1973 than in 1986. Neither wife's age, size of family, nor home ownership influenced pre-tax or after-tax income.

In analyzing the effect of the independent variables on family assets, we found that wife's employment status does not influence household holdings of the financial assets studied. The F-test result for the first hypothesis for wife's age was 40.22, for family composition 8.51, and for home ownership 21.43, which were all significant at the .0001 level.

Examining the impact of these variables over time (Table 7.2), wife's employment status did not influence family assets in either 1972–1973 or 1986. In contrast to the findings for income, wife's age, family composition, and home ownership were significant for household assets, and the impacts differed between 1972–1973 and 1986. When wife's age was less than thirty-five, assets declined more in 1972–1973 than in 1986. In families with no children or two children, assets increased more in 1972–1973 than in 1986; but for families with one child, assets increased in 1972–1973 and decreased in 1986. Home ownership influenced assets differently in the two periods: owners both with and without mortgages had greater financial assets in 1972–1973 than in 1986.

Results of ANOVA. The income and asset data were further analyzed by ANOVA, and the results in Table 7.3 support the results of regression

Table 7.2
Regression of Wife's Work Status, Wife's Age, Family Composition, and Home Ownership on Income and Assets, 1972–1973 and 1986

Independent Variable	Pre-tax Income[a]			After-tax Income[b]			Assets[c]		
	1972–73	1986	F	1972–73	1986	F	1972–73	1986	F
Wife's Work Status									
Full-time	$8415	$4234	7.37*	$6617	$3807	4.66*	$84	-$1636	0.86
Part-time	3933	255	5.47*	3170	523	3.96*	-452	1434	0.99
Age									
Less than 35	-7712	-7126	0.20	-6061	-5899	0.02	-9544	-3909	12.52*
Family Composition									
No children	-659	1385	1.39	-2536	156	3.37	10667	1469	19.38*
1 child	248	147	0.00	-1202	-182	0.48	5855	-348	8.79*
2 children	3271	3580	0.03	1637	2705	0.53	5590	192	6.75*
Home Ownership									
Mortgage	11272	11888	0.18	9173	10960	2.15	6666	1894	7.59*
No mortgage	8479	6494	1.15	65467	6075	0.09	12601	2787	19.35*

[a]R-square=0.8074, $F_{16,107}$=28.04, p=0.0001.
[b]R-square=0.8020, $F_{16,107}$=27.084, p=0.0001.
[c]R-square=0.7429, $F_{16,107}$=19.322, p=0.0001.
*p<.05.

Table 7.3
ANOVA for Comparison of Income and Assets by Wife's Work Status, 1972–1973 and 1986

Income and Assets	Sum of Squares	df	F	P-value	Scheffe's Test F-P	F-N	P-N
1972-1973							
Pre-tax Income	37,060,261,191	2	63.92	0.0001	*	*	*
After-tax Income	19,814,290,855	2	52.47	0.0001	*	*	*
Assets	7,688,471,968	2	2.83	0.0593			
1986							
Pre-tax Income	25,806,752,174	2	41.19	0.0001	*	*	
After-tax Income	17,202,233,757	2	33.79	0.0001	*	*	*
Assets	778,157,388	2	1.68	0.1865			

*p < 0.05.

analysis for full-time and part-time working wives. For families with a nonworking wife, her work status significantly influenced pre-tax income in 1972–1973 and 1986, and after-tax income in 1986. Wife's work status in the three family types did not significantly influence financial assets.

There are significant differences among the three types of working-wife families in both pre-tax and after-tax income in 1972–1973 and 1986, except for pre-tax income in 1986 between PWW and NWW families. There are several possible explanations for this exception. It may indicate greater income comparability between PWW and NWW families in 1986 than in the earlier period, or that in 1986 part-time-working wives contributed less to family pre-tax income than in 1972–1973. The findings for 1986 differ between pre-tax and after-tax income, which was not the case in 1972–1973. This may reflect changes in the impact of income tax on the two types of families.

In the comparison of family assets, wife's work status had no significant influence on assets for either period. Since no significant differences in total family assets were found, we analyzed the four types of financial assets separately. The only two significant differences between family types were in 1972–1973: (1) FWW families had significantly higher checking account balances than PWW families, and (2) NWW families had significantly higher savings accounts than PWW families, but not higher than FWW families. In 1986, the three types of families were more similar in their holdings of these four major assets; there were no significant differences between households. This implies that wife's employment

Table 7.4
ANOVA for Comparison of Assets by Wife's Work Status by Income Level, 1972–1973 and 1986

Income Level	Sum of Squares	df	F	P-value	Scheffe's Test F-P	F-N	P-N
1972-1973							
$10- 20,000	48,063,461	2	0.50	0.6044			
20- 40,000	5,353,289,530	2	6.29	0.0019		*	
40- 60,000	20,072,172,889	2	6.24	0.0020		*	
60-100,000	6,561,618,001	2	0.79	0.4560			
1986							
$10- 20,000	18,191,722	2	0.48	0.6168			
20- 40,000	494,372,223	2	5.16	0.0059	*		
40- 60,000	3,067,629,920	2	6.16	0.0022	*		
60-100,000	116,522,331	2	0.07	0.9367			

*p < 0.05.

status is not the determinant of family assets, which reinforces the similar finding in the regression analysis.

We also analyzed assets by wife's work status and by family income level (Table 7.4). The only significant difference in assets occurred for middle-income ($20,000 to $60,000) families, but with different results in the two periods. In 1972–1973, the difference was between FWW and NWW families, but in 1986 it was between families with full-time and part-time working wives.

Summary and Conclusions

Changes in wives' employment status substantially affected incomes and financial resources of families with working wives relative to those with nonworking wives. This is demonstrated by our comparative analysis of the income and assets of one-earner and dual-earner families. The broad issue is whether wives' income compensated for the stagnation of wages and real income during the period 1972–1973 to 1986.

Overall, we find pre-tax income (in constant dollars) declined for all family types from 1972–1973 to 1986, and after-tax income declined for families with part-time working and nonworking wives, but not for those with full-time working wives. The pre-tax earned income data are significantly different between FWW and PWW, and also between FWW and

NWW families, in both 1972–1973 and 1986. The case is less clear between PWW and NWW families, where pre-tax income and household earnings differed significantly in 1972–1973 but not in 1986, indicating greater income comparability between these two family types in 1986 than in 1972–1973.

Income after tax differed significantly between the three types of families in both 1972–1973 and 1986. Families with full-time working wives differed significantly from the other two types in total tax paid in both 1972–1973 and 1986. However, PWW and NWW families did not differ significantly from each other in either period. Dual-earner FWW families were the only group to have increases in mean after-tax income over this period of stagnant wage growth. This indicates that over time they will continue to diverge from the other two family types. In addition to the increase in nominal family income due to wife's employment, an additional and potentially important factor is the stability of income or safety net added by having a second worker when one spouse is ill or unemployed (Rubin 1982; Michael 1985; Blank 1988).

One of the most interesting findings is the substantial decline in mean financial assets of all three types of married-couple families from 1972–1973 to 1986. The decreases were larger for FWW and NWW than for PWW families. This asset reduction may reflect the income declines associated with slowed productivity gains and decreased real incomes over the study period. Alternatively, it may result from families' attempts to maintain standards of living in the face of slower economic growth and even stagnation, by reducing their marginal propensity to save. This is consistent with Wolff's (1989) finding of a declining propensity to save. As family size increases for all family types, the decline in assets reflects the high cost of rearing children (especially the large decreases from childless couples to those with children). This indicates that children are a consumption good rather than an investment good.

These findings have implications for policy as well as for household decision making. In particular, our findings are relevant for tax policies that impact married-couple families and savings. This evidence supports the case for increased support for working wives, and for policies to promote household savings.

APPENDIX

In the empirical section, we analyze the impact of wife's employment status and other independent variables on pre-tax and after-tax income and assets of married-couple families. The data and methodology for this analysis are detailed below.

Data and Methodology

Pre-tax and after-tax income and four types of asset data were developed from the CE interview tapes for cross-sectional analysis of the periods 1972–1973 and 1986. Money income of households is the pre-tax cash income received from all sources, including labor and nonlabor earnings. All 1972–1973 data were inflated by multiplying by the constant value 2.54, based on a Consumer Price Index of 129.2 for 1972–1973 and of 328.4 for 1986.[6]

CE data for 1972–1973 and 1986 were sorted by categories of wife's employment status (three), age (two), family size (four), and home ownership (three) to obtain mean data on income and assets for each of the seventy-two possible cells. Cells that contained fewer than six families were excluded as too small for analysis, leaving sixty-six cells for 1972–1973 and fifty-eight cells for 1986. In attempting to use income level as an additional independent variable in the analysis of assets, we found insufficient cells that were large enough for analysis. However, four income-level categories were used in the ANOVA to compare assets by wife's employment status for 1972–1973 and 1986.

We examined pre-tax and after-tax income and holdings of the selected assets for the three types of wife's employment status by income level and by family size, for the two time periods. We applied two statistical tests to the data sets: regression analysis and ANOVA.

Regression Analysis

We applied regression analysis to determine the impact of four independent variables—wife's employment status (W), wife's age (A), family composition (F), and home ownership (H)—on the dependent variables of pre-tax income, after-tax income, and assets, at the .05 level of significance. The general form of the regression model is

$$Y_i = f(W, A, F, H),$$

where

Y_i =   pre-tax income, if i = 1; after-tax income, if i = 2; household assets, if i = 3.

The detailed regression model, with all independent variables of each period recoded as dummy variables, is

$$Y_i = a + b_1W1 + b_2W2 + b_3W3 + b_4W4 + b_5A1 + b_6A2 + b_7F1$$
$$+ b_8F2 + b_9F3 + b_{10}F4 + b_{11}F5 + b_{12}F6 + b_{13}H1 + b_{14}H2$$
$$+ b_{15}H3 + b_{16}H4 + u,$$

where

$W1$ = 1 if full-time employed wife in 1972–1973; 0 if 1986

$W2$ = if full-time employed wife in 1986; 0 if 1972–1973

$W3$ = 1 if part-time employed wife in 1972–1973; 0 if 1986

$W4$ = 1 if part-time employed wife in 1986; 0 if 1972–1973

$A1$ = 1 if wife's age < 35 in 1972–1973; 0 if 1986

$A2$ = 1 if wife's age < 35 in 1986; 0 if 1972–1973

$F1$ = 1 if family size = 2 in 1972–1973; 0 if 1986

$F2$ = 1 if family size = 2 in 1986; 0 if 1972–1973

$F3$ = 1 if family size = 3 in 1972–1973; 0 if 1986

$F4$ = 1 if family size = 3 in 1986; 0 if 1972–1973

$F5$ = 1 if family size = 4 in 1972–1973; 0 if 1986

$F6$ = 1 if family size = 4 in 1986; 0 if 1972–1973

$H1$ = 1 if homeowner with mortgage in 1972–1973; 0 if 1986

$H2$ = 1 if homeowner with mortgage in 1986; 0 if 1972–1973

$H3$ = 1 if homeowner without mortgage in 1972–1973; 0 if 1986

$H4$ = 1 if homeowner without mortgage in 1986; 0 if 1972–1973

u = random error term.

ANOVA

The second statistic used was ANOVA, to compare means of income and assets data for the three family types. If significant differences were found at the .05 level, the Scheffe multiple-range test was employed to determine the significant pair (Bornstedt and Knoke 1982).

NOTES

1. In census data, four-fifths of all tabulated income derives from wages, salaries, and self-employment income (Levy 1988b). We find that proportion to be approximately 90 percent in this study, because we exclude most transfer payments.

2. While housing equity is recognized as the major personal investment of most U.S. households, such data are not available in the Consumer Expenditure Survey.

3. Our findings on wife's earnings as a share of total family income from the Consumer Expenditure Survey for 1972–1973 are consistent with those reported by Bell (1976) from the Current Population Reports for 1971.

4. Note that the category "childless couple" may encompass very different groups, such as young couples without children and mature households with no or grown children. Based on their different positions in the life cycle, one would expect very different income/asset relationships between these households.

5. All of these were significant at the .0001 level, except family composition, which was significant at the .001 level.

6. Inflating CE data to 1986 constant dollars, Lazear and Michael (1986) used a factor of 3.7 for 1960–1961 data and 2.5 for 1972–1973 data.

8

Wives' Employment and the Distribution of Income

While the dramatic rise in wives' labor force participation increased incomes of individual families, the growth of dual-earner families also significantly affected the distribution and degree of inequality of family income. The number of earners per family affects the national distribution and equality of income. Family composition is among the most important factors affecting the degree of inequality in household income, emphasizing the need to assess the impact of changes in families on inequality. Increased employment of wives and the growth of dual-earner families have been a dominant factor in changing income distribution.

The impact of wives' earnings on income distribution and its equality is not as straightforward as it might appear. Historically, wives whose husbands were low earners had much higher rates of employment than other wives. This had an equalizing effect on income distribution. However, as increased numbers of wives entered the labor force, other factors have overcome this equalizing effect. Wives of higher-earning spouses are likely to have higher levels of education and more employment resources, and thus also to be higher earners. As their employment increases, income distribution becomes less equal.

Wives' employment status and whether they are employed full-time and full-year, rather than part-time, also determines the impact on equality. Three-fourths of employed wives (22 million) worked full-time in 1991, with the remaining fourth (8 million) working part-time (U.S. Department of Labor, Bureau of Labor Statistics 1991). These relative shares have remained quite stable since 1960, with less than 2 percent change over each decade. Of full-time employed wives, a large share worked full-year, while only a small share of those employed part-time worked full-year. Wife's employment status is clearly a determinant of total family earnings. In 1990, dual-earner family earnings were $55,068 when both worked full-time and year-round. Earnings were $39,083 when the husband worked full-time and the wife was not employed, almost the same as the $39,895 average earnings for all married couples (U.S. Bureau of the Census 1992).

The objective of this chapter is to analyze characteristics of income distribution and inequality among different groups of married-couple families, with emphasis on wife's work status. The next section provides background on the basic conceptual issues of the economics of income distribution and inequality, followed by an overview of previous studies in this area. We then present an empirical analysis of the equality of income distribution for various groups of married-couple families. Specifically, we look at both pre-tax and after-tax incomes of dual-earner and single-earner families and also distinguish between full-time and part-time employed wives. We conclude with policy implications of working wives for income distribution and equity.

MEASURES OF INCOME DISTRIBUTION AND INEQUALITY

The distribution of income refers to the relative share of total income obtained by different groups in the population. Among households, income equality indicates receipt of an equal percent of total income, usually by each quintile (one-fifth) of the population. A graphic representation, the Lorenz curve, is used to present income distribution and its degree of inequality. To construct a Lorenz curve, the percentage share of income received is plotted against the percentage share of families. Income is equally distributed when any given percent of families receives an equal percent of the total income (e.g., each 20 percent of families receives 20 percent of the income), as represented by a straight 45° line of equality. However, the actual distribution of income, as depicted by the Lorenz curve, deviates from this straight line of equality. The extent of this deviation measures the degree of inequality, so the Lorenz curve shows actual money income received in relation to (or as a deviation from) perfectly equal distribution.

The extent of inequality of income distribution is measured by a Gini coefficient. The Gini coefficient compares the area between the 45° line of perfectly equal income distribution and the Lorenz curve of actual income distribution. A Gini ratio of 0 indicates perfect equality of incomes, so the Lorenz curve is the same as the line of equality. A Gini ratio of 1 represents perfect inequality, so the lower the Gini value, the more equal the distribution of income.

Since World War II, the distribution of income of American families has remained remarkably stable. The income share received by each quintile of families has changed little during this period of major economic growth and change. Thus, an appropriate question concerns the impact of the significant increase in employed wives on income distribution. The answer is not that wives' movement into the labor force has caused the distribution of income to improve. Instead, this shift has prevented other factors from causing deterioration in the equality of the distribution of income (Wion 1990). As noted in Chapter 2, wives' increased employment and earnings have offset the declining labor force participation of men, the increased dispersion (greater inequality) in men's earnings, and, by the 1970s, the reduced growth of men's real wages.

FAMILY INCOME DISTRIBUTION AND INEQUALITY

Most studies analyzing the impact of wives' earnings on income distribution and inequality have emphasized their contribution to married-couple families rather than to all households. Some of these studies used total family income, while others used earnings of husband and wife, or family income and wife's earnings. These empirical studies also vary in the data base used, the methodology for measuring inequality, and the time frame. Despite these differences, the research findings are unanimous on the central point that wives' earnings enhance equality of the distribution of family pre-tax income, particularly for white families.

In his seminal work, Mincer (1962) discussed the negative relation between labor force participation rates of wives and income of husband, which reduced household income inequality. Later, he developed the analysis of husband's and wife's earnings and the relationship between them. This formally showed the derivation of family income inequality as the sum of the variances in inequality in the earnings distributions of husbands and wives plus the covariance between them (see also Treas 1987; Wion 1990). Mincer concluded that the growth of women's labor force participation was a factor in reducing income inequality among families.

Using 1960 census data, Sweet (1971) analyzed income distribution and inequality. His Gini coefficient results indicated husbands' income was less equitably distributed than family income, and "the effect of differential employment and earnings patterns of wives makes an insignificant difference to the inequality of distribution of income" (Sweet 1971, p. 407). He further found the income of family earners other than the wife had a greater effect on income inequality between blacks and whites than did wife's employment.

Studies of the equalizing impact of wives' employment have found different effects by race. Analyzing wives' earnings and the distribution of family income by race, with 1960 and 1970 census data, Smith (1979) corroborated Mincer's findings for white, but not for black, families. He found wives' earnings equalized income in white families but increased inequality among black families. He also noted that husbands in dual-earner families had lower wages than the average for all husbands. Smith concluded that white family members use wife's labor supply adjustments as a compensatory function to maintain total family income. This was corroborated by Rubin and Gilbert (1976), who found that working wives in the 1960s and 1970s tended to be in low-income families because their spouses were very low earners.

The impact of wives' increased labor supply on the distribution of household income was analyzed by Betson and van der Gaag (1984), using Current Population Survey (CPS) data for 1968 to 1980. They found the large increase in employed wives was a major factor in the reduction of income inequality. However, the impact differed by race, with wives' earnings decreasing inequality between one- and two-earner households for nonblack families but increasing inequality among black families. They concluded that wives' earnings were an increasingly important equalizing factor in total household income distribution.

Danziger (1980) also concluded that wives' earnings have a small equalizing effect on the distribution of family income in his analysis of CPS data for 1967 and 1974. He found that wives' earnings remained relatively stable during the study period, at 27 percent of income for white families with working wives and 33 percent for nonwhite families. However, wives' earnings accounted for about 20 percent of family income at the lowest end of the distribution and only 5 percent at the top. The Gini coefficient for whites was 5 percent lower than it would have been without wives' earnings; for nonwhites, wives' earnings did not affect the coefficient.

In a review of female labor force participation and household income, Michael (1985) noted the need for further analysis of wives' earnings within husband-wife families and also of differences between household groups. Bryant and Zick (1986), using 1979–1980 data from the Panel Study of Income Dynamics for white husband-wife families, concluded that wives' earnings reduced the Gini ratio by 10 percent. They found a greater effect on the economic well-being of their families from the employment of women in low-income than in high-income households. Minarik (1988) further supported the equalizing impact of wives' employment. He concluded that among married-couple families, the increase in the number of working wives has decreased inequality of income distribution.

Thurow (1980) noted that working wives increase equality because their earnings are much more equally distributed than their husbands'. However, he predicted that we were entering a period of rising income inequality because of changes in female work patterns. Thurow's prediction was corroborated by Blank (1988), using 1985 CPS data. In contrast to earlier findings, Blank (1988) found that husbands with working wives generally had higher earnings than husbands who were only-earners, so that dual earnings increased the relative position of already better-off families. She reported that married-couple families with working wives were twice as likely to be in the top quintile of the income distribution of households overall, with 40 percent in this group and only 3 percent in the lowest fifth. In a Brookings Institution study, Levy (1988b) concurred, concluding that the share of families with incomes over $50,000 increased, primarily due to the increasing number of dual-earner families. He found a fourth of dual-earner families with incomes over $50,000 (in constant 1987 dollars) in both 1973 and 1986. Since the proportion of households with two incomes has grown, the share of the income distribution at that level has increased correspondingly. In a dissenting longitudinal analysis, Wion (1990) employed simulations based on CPS data for 1967–1984 to study the impact of working wives' income on inequality. He found a neutral effect on the distribution of married couples' earnings and concluded that increases in inequality were little affected by changes in the proportion of working wives.

These studies demonstrate that the impact of wives' earnings shifted over time to become an increasingly important factor in family income distribution and inequality. Overall, the increase in wives' labor force participation had an equalizing effect for white families but an unequalizing effect for nonwhites (Sweet 1980; Michael 1985). However, there is evidence that as more wives in upper-income households expand their labor force participation, the inequality of income distribution for married-couple families will increase.

In the following study, we contribute to this issue by disaggregating the work status of wives into full-time and part-time and by using other demographic variables. We analyzed the income distribution of dual-earner and single-earner married couples, and incorporated additional labor force information by distinguishing wives' full-time and part-time employment status.

FAMILY INCOME DISTRIBUTION: EMPIRICAL ANALYSIS[1]

This empirical analysis compares income distribution and inequality among different groups of married-couple families, with emphasis on wife's work status. To extend previous findings, we distinguished between full-time and part-time work status of wives. The study addressed three questions: (1) Do wife's work status and various demographic variables have an impact on the distribution of income both before and after taxes, and if so, how? (2) How do wife's work status and various demographic variables affect mean income both before and after taxes? (3) In particular, how do wife's work status, race, region, family size, and husband's occupation affect the equality of family income distribution and mean income?

Data and Methodology

The data base is from the 1986 Consumer Expenditure Survey (CE), discussed in Chapter 1. Data sets for both pre-tax and after-tax measures of family income were constructed from the CE sample and ordered cumulatively by size of family income. Income in the CE consists of household income from all sources, including earnings and the return to assets; after-tax income is income after all federal, state, and local taxes. In particular, use of the CE enabled us to analyze after-tax income, which is not possible for income distribution studies based on the more widely used Current Population Survey (CPS). Taking taxes into account provided a clearer picture of income distribution because gains from wives' employment are otherwise overstated (Treas 1987). In addition to family income, we used five explanatory demographic variables: wife's work status, race, region, family size, and four aggregated occupational categories of husband.

The data sets were limited to complete income reporters and nonaged (less than age sixty-five) married-couple families. We included only families in which the husband worked full-time; the wife worked full-time (FWW) or part-time (PWW) or was not employed (NWW); and there were no other earners. These criteria produced a pre-tax income data set of 5,909 observations and an after-tax income data set of 5,937 observations.[2]

The methodology had three steps. First, the pre-tax and after-tax income data sets were ordered by size of income to construct Lorenz curve-type data sets. From these, we developed income distributions for family groups with different characteristics. Utilizing these two ordered data sets, we constructed five additional subgroup models (for both the pre-tax and after-tax data), with one of the demographic groups dropped, one at a time, in each of these models. For example, both the pre-tax and after-tax models were constructed to include all of the demographic variables except family size.

Second, to analyze the degree of income inequality, the Gini coefficient (G) was computed to measure the inequality of income distribution for families with different demographic and economic characteristics. Then we applied regression analysis to examine the impact of the explanatory variables on the Gini coefficients of inequality.

Third, to analyze mean income, a method analogous to the second step was developed, but we used a measure of mean income rather than the Gini coefficient of inequality. Each group mean income was regressed against the same independent demographic variables. The detailed methodology for this study and the regression models are presented in the appendix.

Findings

The regression estimates for the impact of wife's work status and the other demographic variables on the Gini coefficients indicate inequality in the distribution of income. Table 8.1 shows the estimates for before-tax income and Table 8.2 shows those for income after taxes. The corresponding regression results for the impact of these independent variables on mean family income before taxes are presented in Table 8.3 and for mean after-tax income in Table 8.4.

The results for the entire model, with all five groups of independent variables included, are in column 1 of tables 8.1–8.4. Columns 2–6 of the four tables show the regression results for the five variants of the model, with each of these decreased by one different group of demographic variables. This approach reduced the total number of cells but increased the size of each cell (as seen by N1 and N2 in each table). The effects of the explanatory factors were examined, using these reduced models. In other words, in tables 8.1–8.4, for the regression model results shown in column 2, family size is not observed; for column 3, husband's occupation is deleted; for column 4, region; for column 5, race; and for column 6, wife's work status is omitted.

Table 8.1
Regression Results for Gini Coefficients: Impact of Wife's Employment Status on the Distribution of Before-Tax Income, 1986

Independent Variables	Models					
	(1)	(2)	(3)	(4)	(5)	(6)
Intercept	0.273	0.318	0.340	0.346	0.284	0.272
	(13.65)a	(12.49)a	(12.80)a	(12.98)a	(17.24)a	(11.10)b
Wife's Employment Status						
Full-Time	-0.059	-0.063	-0.087	-0.069	-0.060	*excluded*
	(-4.34)a	(-3.17)a	(-4.00)a	(-3.14)a	(-4.90)a	
Part-Time	-0.005	0.022	0.058	0.059	-0.004	*excluded*
	(-0.37)	(1.00)	(2.45)b	(2.60)b	(-0.30)	
Race						
White	0.014	-0.043	-0.098	-0.067	*excluded*	-0.041
	(0.97)	(-2.49)a	(-5.07)a	(-3.67)a		(-2.47)b
Region						
Northeast	0.031	0.024	0.019	*excluded*	0.011	0.034
	(1.89)c	(0.98)	(0.70)		(0.79)	(1.41)
Midwest	0.012	-0.006	-0.013	*excluded*	-0.011	0.016
	(0.77)	(-0.27)	(-0.51)		(-0.81)	(0.70)
South	0.032	0.013	-0.012	*excluded*	0.012	0.013
	(2.15)b	(0.56)	(0.51)		(0.86)	(0.60)
Husband's Occupation						
Managerial	-0.018	-0.059	*excluded*	-0.041	-0.0002	-0.038
	(-1.17)	(-2.61)b		(-1.65)	(-0.02)	(-1.69)c
Technical	-0.027	-0.038	*excluded*	-0.030	-0.006	-0.022
	(-1.70)c	(-1.60)		(-1.19)	(-0.42)	(-0.98)
Service	0.048	0.049	*excluded*	0.025	0.082	0.075
	(3.07)a	(2.08)b		(0.97)	(5.76)a	(3.19)b
Family Size						
No Children	0.009	*excluded*	0.012	-0.041	0.009	-0.005
	(0.70)		(0.56)	(-1.96)c	(0.70)	(-0.27)
One Child	-0.002	*excluded*	0.018	-0.009	0.001	0.006
	(-0.11)		(0.82)	(0.38)	(0.10)	(0.32)
R^2	0.27	0.38	0.54	0.50	0.41	0.30
N1	288	96	72	72	144	96
N2	184	82	60	64	140	85

Notes: Number in parentheses is the t-ratio; a = significant at $p < 0.01$ level; b = significant at $p < 0.05$ level; c = significant at $p < 0.10$ level; N1 = maximum number of cells; N2 = number of cells with more than five observations.

Distribution of Income Before Taxes. For the before-tax model (column 1 of Table 8.1), utilizing all the demographic variables indicates that the coefficient for wife's full-time work status (FWW) is negative and significant (at the .01 level). Thus, within the sample population of full-time working wives the level of income inequality is lower than within the

Table 8.2

Regression Results for Gini Coefficient: Impact of Wife's Employment Status on the Distribution of After-Tax Income, 1986

Independent Variables	Models					
	(1)	(2)	(3)	(4)	(5)	(6)
Intercept	0.289	0.331	0.343	0.347	0.282	0.265
	(14.59)a	(12.88)a	(12.3)a	(12.14)a	(16.90)a	(10.78)b
Wife's Employment Status						
Full-Time	-0.065	-0.065	-0.094	-0.072	-0.057	*excluded*
	(-4.86)a	(-3.27)a	(-4.15)a	(-3.08)a	(-4.63)a	
Part-Time	-0.024	0.009	0.041	0.046	-0.011	*excluded*
	(-1.61)	(0.41)	(1.66)	(1.87)c	(-0.86)	
Race						
White	0.006	-0.054	-0.102	-0.071	*excluded*	-0.047
	(0.42)	(-3.07)a	(-5.06)a	(-3.61)a		(-2.83)a
Region						
Northeast	0.035	0.019	0.023	*excluded*	0.024	0.037
	(2.18)b	(0.77)	(0.81)		(1.65)	(1.52)
Midwest	0.007	-0.002	-0.012	*excluded*	-0.002	0.011
	(0.43)	(-0.10)	(-0.44)		(-0.17)	(0.46)
South	0.027	0.0001	-0.013	*excluded*	0.015	0.013
	(1.85)c	(0.004)	(0.60)		(1.08)	(0.58)
Husband's Occupation						
Managerial	-0.016	-0.057	*excluded*	-0.032	0.004	-0.025
	(-1.09)	(-2.50)b		(-1.19)	(0.29)	(-1.13)
Technical	-0.032	-0.032	*excluded*	-0.028	-0.014	-0.005
	(-2.04)b	(-1.32)		(-1.04)	(-0.95)	(-0.20)
Service	0.034	0.043	*excluded*	0.019	0.072	0.077
	(2.21)b	(1.83)c		(0.69)	(4.97)a	(3.29)a
Family Size						
No Children	0.006	*excluded*	0.014	-0.044	0.003	-0.008
	(0.48)		(0.59)	(-1.95)c	(0.26)	(-0.40)
One Child	-0.004	*excluded*	0.025	-0.014	-0.006	0.007
	(-0.32)		(1.07)	(0.55)	(-0.51)	(0.37)
R^2	0.24	0.36	0.51	0.44	0.35	0.28
N1	288	96	72	72	144	96
N2	184	82	60	64	140	85

Notes: Number in parentheses is the t-ratio; a = significant at $p < 0.01$ level; b = significant at $p < 0.05$ level; c = significant at $p < 0.10$ level; N1 = maximum number of cells; N2 = number of cells with more than five observations.

population of nonworking wives, holding all other factors constant. This indicates that if nonworking wives begin to work full-time, the degree of equality of family income distribution is expected to increase.

The coefficient for part-time working wives (PWW), while negative, is not significant. Thus, part-time working wives do not significantly reduce

Table 8.3
Regression Results for Impact of Wife's Employment Status on Mean Income Before Taxes, 1986

Independent Variables	Models					
	(1)	(2)	(3)	(4)	(5)	(6)
Intercept	25446	24020	31278	20530	24237	25689
	(16.90)a	(15.84)a	(15.92)a	(14.25)a	(19.57)a	(18.28)a
Wife's Employment Status						
Full-Time	8684	8704	7593	9419	7302	excluded
	(8.51)a	(7.37)a	(4.74)a	(7.96)a	(7.94)a	
Part-Time	945	-659	-1453	1164	1143	excluded
	(0.84)	(-0.52)	(0.84)	(-0.95)	(1.23)	
Race						
White	1870	4764	4170	3357	excluded	2267
	(1.76)c	(4.60)a	(2.93)a	(3.38)a		(2.37)b
Region						
Northeast	-4929	-5311	-4784	excluded	-1691	-3183
	(-4.01)a	(-3.70)a	(-2.37)b		(-1.57)	(-2.31)b
Midwest	-4862	-4177	-2954	excluded	-2732	-4306
	(-4.15)a	(-2.96)a	(-1.54)		(-2.58)b	(-3.31)a
South	-3755	-4305	-5052	excluded	-1950	-3276
	(-3.33)a	(-3.21)a	(-2.81)a		(-1.86)c	(-2.66)a
Husband's Occupation						
Managerial	15955	15425	excluded	15620	14858	15425
	(13.88)a	(11.54)a		(11.55)a	(14.16)a	(12.09)a
Technical	7439	7102	excluded	8031	5829	7532
	(6.27)a	(4.98)a		(5.94)a	(5.51)a	(5.76)a
Service	97	-375	excluded	627	1112	2042
	(0.08)	(-0.27)		(0.46)	(1.04)	(1.52)
Family Size						
No Children	647	excluded	787	17701	-266	2141
	(0.63)		(0.48)	(1.54)	(-0.29)	(1.86)c
One Child	-619	excluded	-1286	-335	-1327	42
	(-0.60)		(-0.78)	(-0.27)	(-1.43)	(0.04)
R^2	0.68	0.79	0.5	0.83	0.72	0.72
N1	288	96	72	72	144	96
N2	184	82	60	64	140	85

Notes: Number in parentheses is the t-ratio; a = significant at $p < 0.01$ level; b = significant at $p < 0.05$ level; c = significant at $p < 0.10$ level; N1 = maximum number of cells; N2 = number of cells with more than five observations.

inequality of the distribution of income, compared with nonworking wives. This is of interest because the results for full-time working wives support Mincer's (1962) findings, while those for part-time do not. One explanation of these results is that PWW families are more similar to NWW than to FWW families. This may occur because the income gener-

Table 8.4

Regression Results for Impact of Wife's Employment Status on Mean Income After Taxes, 1986

Independent Variables	Models					
	(1)	(2)	(3)	(4)	(5)	(6)
Intercept	22677	21200	28417	18932	24237	25689
	(15.41)a	(14.35)a	(15.61)a	(13.45)a	(19.57)a	(18.28)a
Wife's Employment Status						
Full-Time	7261	7237	6263	8260	7302	*excluded*
	(7.28)a	(6.29)a	(4.22)a	(7.15)a	(7.94)a	
Part-Time	1201	−562	−1000	−778	1143	*excluded*
	(1.10)	(−0.45)	(−0.62)	(−0.65)	(1.23)	
Race						
White	2027	4472	4036	3490	*excluded*	2267
	(2.00)b	(4.43)a	(3.06)a	(3.60)a		(2.37)b
Region						
Northeast	−3293	−3243	−2802	*excluded*	−1690	−3183
	(−2.74)a	(−2.32)b	(−1.50)		(−1.57)	(−2.31)b
Midwest	−3873	−2819	−1671	*excluded*	−2732	−4306
	(−3.38)a	(−2.05)b	(−0.94)		(−2.58)b	(−3.31)a
South	−2565	−2878	−3676	*excluded*	−1950	−3276
	(−2.33)b	(−2.20)b	(−2.21)b		(−1.86)c	(−2.66)a
Husband's Occupation						
Managerial	15417	14666	*excluded*	14780	14858	15425
	(13.72)a	(11.26)a		(11.19)a	(14.16)a	(12.09)a
Technical	6467	6273	*excluded*	7022	5829	7532
	(5.58)a	(4.52)a		(5.31)a	(5.51)a	(5.76)a
Service	1640	1050	*excluded*	1508	1112	2042
	(1.42)	(0.77)		(1.12)	(1.04)	(1.52)
Family Size						
No Children	235	*excluded*	262	1013	−266	2141
	(0.24)		(0.72)	(1.91)	(−0.30)	(1.86)c
One Child	−1248	*excluded*	−1818	−1003	−1327	42
	(−1.24)		(−1.19)	(−0.83)	(−1.43)	(0.04)
R^2	0.63	0.76	0.45	0.81	0.72	0.72
N1	288	96	72	72	144	96
N2	184	82	60	64	140	85

Notes: Number in parentheses is the t-ratio; a = significant at $p < 0.01$ level; b = significant at $p < 0.05$ level; c = significant at $p < 0.10$ level; N1 = maximum number of cells; N2 = number of cells with more than five observations.

ated by the part-time working wife is either temporary or too small to be significant. This result confirms the hypothesis of Thurow (1980) that as long as some wives work full-time and others part-time, the equality of income will tend to decrease, since the two have different impacts on the distribution of family income. Our finding may also explain some of the contradictions found by those studying the impact of wives' income on the distribution of income. For instance, the difference in the findings of Danziger (1980) compared with those of Blank (1988), Minarik (1988), and Levy (1988b), or even the neutralizing impact shown by Wion (1990), may occur because these researchers did not discriminate between full-time and part-time working wives.

Looking at the regional variable, location in the Northeast or South was positive and significant (at the .10 and .05 levels, respectively). This indicates that residence in these areas, compared with residence in the West, leads to greater inequality of income distribution. Husband's occupation had varying impacts on equality of income distribution of married-couple families.

Columns 2–6 of Table 8.1 show the results for the five model variations, with a different demographic variable deleted from each model to examine the impacts of the other variables in a less disaggregated model. For each of the reduced models where wife's full-time employment status was present (for the models represented in columns 2–5), wife's full-time work showed the same effect of increasing equality of income distribution (p < .01) as for the complete model. Only for the models without the regional and the husband's occupation variables (columns 4 and 3) was wife's part-time work status significant (p < .05), and then it was in the opposite direction, showing increasing inequality, which once again contradicted the findings of Mincer (1962). Further, the reduced model with the least R^2 is shown in column 6, where wife's work status is not included.

Race was significant (at the .01 level for all models except the one where wife's work status is deleted) with a negative coefficient for each of the models. This occurred when the number of observations in each cell was increased by reducing the number of variables. Thus, being white increased equality of income distribution, compared with being nonwhite. This supports the findings of Smith (1979) and Betson and van der Gaag (1984).

Husband's occupation category of services, farming, armed forces, or self-employed (O3) was significant and positive in all cases except when region was omitted (column 4). This indicates that husband's occupation contributed to increased inequality of income distribution. Husband's occupation of technical or sales (category O2) was significant but negative for the full model, as shown in column 1. Husband's occupation of managerial or professional (category O1) was also significant but negative for the models without the family size and wife's work status variables. This suggests that regardless of the working status of the wife, the husband's occupation remains a significant factor altering the distribution of income. Finally, the family size was significant, and negative, for the model in which region was suppressed, and then only for families with no children.

Distribution of Income After Taxes. Table 8.2 represents the six models, as in Table 8.1, but applied to after-tax family income, which few other researchers have studied. The same variables remained significant for after-tax income as for pre-tax income in all but two cases (for PWW in column 3 and for husband's occupation category O1 in column 6), although the level of significance varies. The important similar results for after-tax income are the negative and significant coefficient for full-time working wives, the negative and significant race coefficient for all but the full model, and generally not significant coefficient for family size.

Two interesting differences between pre-tax and after-tax income distributions occurred. The part-time work status of the wife (PWW) did not have the strong impact on income inequality (for the models where husband's occupation or region is dropped) that it did before taxes. This is consistent with previous research, which suggested that the PWW's high opportunity cost reduces the contribution of the wife's income to total family income and therefore lessens the impact on the distribution of income (Rubin et al. 1987). We found a similar impact for husband's occupation category O1, which was significant for the before-tax analysis in the model where wife's work status was dropped and was no longer significant in the after-tax analysis. Further, these results may reflect a cross-correlation between selectivity in which women choose to work full-time or part-time and selectivity in what type of men these women are likely to marry.

Mean Income Before and After Taxes. For the model of mean income before taxes (Table 8.3), the results in column 1 utilizing all the demographic variables show that the coefficient for FWW was positive and significant (p < .01). Thus, full-time employed wives increased average family income, while part-time working wives (PWW) did not. Being white and husband's occupation (categories O1 and O2) also increased average before-tax income, but family size did not have a significant effect. Location in the three regions was significant (p < .01) and negative, indicating that residence in these areas reduced mean income. This result may derive from the exclusion of the higher-income West Coast.

For the four reduced models shown in columns 2–5 of Table 8.3, FWW had the same effect of increasing pre-tax mean income (at the .01 level) as for the complete model; but PWW did not. The other reduced pre-tax model results were highly consistent with the results for the full model. The exceptions were that residence was not significant for the Midwest region in case 3 or for the North in case 5; and family size of no children was positive and significant (p < .10) for case 6, where wife's work status was omitted.

The results for mean after-tax income, in Table 8.4, were almost identical to those described for mean income before taxes. The only exceptions were that residence in the Northeast was no longer significant in case 3, and the level of significance was reduced for a few other regions. Thus, wife's work status and other demographic variables had the same effects on before- and after-tax average levels of income.

Conclusions and Policy Implications

By distinguishing between full-time and part-time work status of wives, we introduce labor market information into the income contribution of working wives both to equality of income distribution and to mean income. The results indicate that the distribution of income is more uniform for FWW families both before and after taxes. This result is similar to the findings of other researchers (Mincer 1962; Smith 1979; Blank 1988; Levy 1988b). In contrast, for PWW families there is little or no impact on the equality of income distribution either before or after taxes. This result is similar to that suggested by Danziger (1980).

While our results for both full-time and part-time working wives were similar to those suggested by others, we emphasize that none of the previous studies introduced the labor information included here. These results are similar to those suggested by Thurow (1980), who intimated that wives' differing labor force status could increase inequality. It is clear from our study that as long as some wives are full-time and others are part-time workers, the inequality of income will increase because the impacts of the two are different. Further, not only do the varied work patterns of wives have different impacts on income distribution, but the work status of wives also has different impacts on both before- and after-tax average income. Full-time working wives increase both mean incomes, but part-time working wives do not.

Race substantially alters the distribution of income in most instances, and affects mean income in all cases. Family size has virtually no significant impact on either income distribution or average income. Geographical location is not a strong determinant of income distribution, but it has a significant negative impact on mean income in most cases. Husband's occupation in category O3 (services, farming, armed forces, or self-employed) has a negative impact on income distribution but no significant impact on mean income. In contrast, husband's occupation in category O1 (managerial or professional) or O2 (technical or sales) consistently raises average income.

The inequality of income distribution differs between the before- and after-tax results, but the results are almost identical for average income before and after taxes. Thus, the tax system does affect the equality of income distribution but does not affect relative mean incomes for families of different work status of wife and various demographic compositions.

The empirical analysis of wives' employment status on equality of income distribution and on average income has important implications for national policy-making. We find that for FWW families, the distribution of income both before and after taxes will be more equal than for NWW families, but this effect does not occur for PWW families. Therefore, the inequality of income distribution, whether before or after taxes, is likely to remain or possibly to increase as long as some wives work full-time and others part-time. We found the same to hold for both pre-tax and after-tax average income. This implies that policies to increase equality of the distribution of income will be more effective if they enable increased numbers of wives to work full-time, rather than part-time, or if they enable increased employment of wives. Such policy measures as increased availability of day care, tax deductions to businesses that provide child care, improved family or maternity leave policies, and/or improved tax benefits to working wives can be expected to improve equality of the distribution of income.

APPENDIX

In the empirical section of Chapter 8, we analyze the impact of wives' employment status on the distribution of income and its degree of inequality for both pre-tax and after-tax income. The data and methodology are detailed below.

Data

Data utilized are from the 1986 Consumer Expenditure Survey (CE) interview tapes.[3] Annualized income data are collected in the second and fifth interviews for each consumer unit in the CE for several measures of income, and are reported in each quarter of the data base. Income in the study ranges from zero to $99,999 because income in the CE data above this level is topcoded to $100,000 to assure anonymity of high-income respondents.

In addition to family income, five explanatory demographic variables are included: (1) wife's work status, with less than thirty-five hours per week indicating part-time (PWW), and thirty-five or more hours per week indicating full-time (FWW); (2) race, indicated by white (WH) or non-white (NW);[4] (3) region, divided into Northeast (N), Midwest (MW), South (S), and West (W); (4) family size of 2 (F1 = no children), 3 (F2 = 1 child), and greater than 3 (F3 = two or more children); and (5) four aggregated occupational categories of husband. Husband's aggregated occupational categories were (1) managerial and professional (O1); (2) technical and sales (O2); (3) service, farming, armed forces, and self-employment (O3); and (4) precision production, operators, and laborers (O4).

Methodology

First, the two income data sets for pre-tax and after-tax income were ordered by size of income (i.e., Lorenz curve data were constructed for both pre-tax and after-tax family income), so that distributions of the ordered income could be developed for family groups with different characteristics. Thus, based on the different combinations of these demographic characteristics, 288 different groups for each of the pre-tax and after-tax data sets were constructed. Utilizing these two ordered data sets, we constructed five additional subgroup models (for both the pre-tax and after-tax data), in each of which one of the demographic groups was dropped, one at a time. For instance, pre-tax and after-tax models were constructed that accounted for all of the demographic variables except family size. In this case, a total of 96 cells was possible instead of the 288 when all demographics were included.

Second, for analysis of the degree of income inequality, we constructed the Gini coefficient (G) measure of income distribution inequality for each of the cells in these twelve models,[5] and without any assumption of the underlying form of the income distribution. This coefficient provides a measure, between 0 and 1, of the degree of income inequality indicated by the Lorenz curve cumulative distribution of income. $G = 0$ indicates perfect equality of income distribution, and $G = 1$ indicates perfect inequality. Consequently, a negative and significant coefficient on any of the independent variables lowers the inequality of income distribution. A positive and significant coefficient indicates a variable with the tendency of decreasing equality.

The Gini coefficient for discrete data free of any assumption of the underlying functional form of the income distribution is (Kakwani 1980, p. 69)

$$G = \frac{\Delta}{2\mu}, \tag{1}$$

where

$$\Delta = [\, n\,(\,n-1)\,]^{-1} \sum_{i=1}^{n} \sum_{j=1}^{n} \mid x_i - x_j \mid,$$

and where μ = mean, n = members in each subgroup, and $x_{i\,or\,j}$ represents the income of the ith or the jth consumer.

From our ranked data sets, we constructed the Gini coefficient for each sample subgroup (i.e., for each of the cells in the twelve models) and then regressed the Gini of that group against the independent variables, which are the characteristics of the sample cells. The models for these two series of regressions are of the form

$$G_{\{before\ taxes\}} = a_0 + a_1 FWW + a_2 PWW + a_3 Wh + a_4 N + a_5 MW \tag{2}$$
$$+ a_6 S + a_7 O1 + a_8 O2 + a_9 O3 + a_{10} F1 + a_{11} F2$$

$$G_{\{after\ taxes\}} = b_0 + b_1 FWW + b_2 PWW + b_3 Wh + b_4 N + b_5 MW \tag{3}$$
$$+ b_6 S + b_7 O1 + b_8 O2 + b_9 O3 + b_{10} F1 + b_{11} F2,$$

where

FWW = 1 if full-time employed wife; 0 otherwise
PWW = 1 if part-time employed wife; 0 otherwise
Wh = 1 if white race; 0 otherwise
N = 1 if reside in Northeast; 0 otherwise
MW = 1 if Midwest; 0 otherwise
S = 1 if South; 0 otherwise
O1 = 1 if husband's occupation is managerial and professional; 0 otherwise
O2 = 1 if husband's occupation is technical and sales; 0 otherwise
O3 = 1 if husband's occupation is service, farming, armed forces, or self-employment; 0 otherwise
F1 = 1 if family size is 2 (married couple with no children); 0 otherwise
F2 = 1 if family size is 3 (married couple with one child); 0 otherwise.

Thus, the base case is a family with a nonemployed wife, is nonwhite, resides in the West region, with husband employed in precision production, operators, or laborers category, and with two or more children.

Third, for analysis of mean income, the regression method was analogous to the above, but we employed a measure of mean income rather than the Gini coefficient of inequality. Each group mean income value was regressed against the same independent demographic variables.

NOTES

1. Portions of this study were presented in a paper titled Wife's work status and the distribution of income, by R. M. Rubin and D. J. Molina, at the Western Economics Association, San Diego (July 1990). We thank Dave Molina for his contribution.

2. The number of pre-tax and after-tax families differed because some households having pre-tax incomes higher than $99,999 became part of the after-tax income sample.

3. There are five quarters of data on the 1986 CE tape because the ending months of 1985 are included in the first quarter of 1986 data reported. All five quarters are included in this study in order to maximize sample size.

4. Further disaggregation by race was attempted in order to analyze black, Asian, and other, as categorized in the CE data, but the sample sizes were too small for analysis when the additional variables were considered.

5. Development of the Gini coefficient was limited to cells with a minimum of five members in that subgroup.

9

Dual-Earner Families

Throughout this book we have differentiated the economics of one-earner and dual-earner families, giving particular attention to the effects of full-time versus part-time employed wives on household decision making. We had two important reasons for our interest in this area. One was the lack of comprehensive research or a major text specifically focused on working wives or dual-earner families. The second was the broad-based socioeconomic transitions that generated and accompanied the rapid growth of dual-earner families. These changes have not been sufficiently acknowledged in policy actions, institutional responses, or even by consumer marketing. Thus, we set out to answer some basic questions about dual-earner families: How does having an employed wife influence family lifestyles? What effects do dual-earners have on the economic security of their households and on the distribution of income? What policy changes need to be implemented to recognize the proliferation of dual-earner families?

Sweeping social and economic changes continue to promote women's and wives' increased employment. With the expansion of job opportunities, women are obtaining higher levels of education, entering the labor force prior to marriage, marrying at later ages, and decreasing the size of their families. Young women enter marriage with a commitment to continue employment, and older married women enter or reenter the labor force. Since the early 1970s wives have entered the labor force in record numbers, regardless of their age or their children's ages. Generally high rates of inflation, in addition to wage stagnation for male workers, generated a period of transition for families. The number of employed wives was increasing, but the number of employed husbands was decreasing. This, coupled with the growing dispersion of men's earnings and the reduced growth of their real wages, was offset only by wives' full-time employment.

FAMILY LIFESTYLES

Family lifestyle, based on income and on tastes and preferences, is generally determined by the production and consumption activities of family members striving to obtain the most satisfaction from the use of their resources. Lifestyles are reflected in family earning and spending. In these terms, we found lifestyle differences between one-earner and dual-earner families, and also between dual-earners with full-time and part-time working wives. On average, dual-earner families have higher levels of education and more mobility, and since they have higher incomes, they are more likely to be home owners and spenders. Whether our research focus was on wife's work status, family income level, family size, or comparisons over time, income was found to be the most important determinant of expenditures.

Many wives work in order to raise household income, alter lifestyles and living standards, and particularly to finance their desired housing. For wife's employment to raise the standard of living, the family should assess the costs and benefits of having two incomes. For dual-earner households, the critical determinants of both husbands' and wives' employment are total income, which defines their tax bracket, and the need for child care. At all income levels, we found that the most important expenditure difference between one- and two-earner households with young children is the cost of child care. At the same level of income, one-earner and dual-earner families have similar spending patterns except for child care and transportation.

It is notable that families of working wives do not use more domestic services than families of nonemployed wives. This suggests that differences in their household production functions derive more from internal family substitution than from replacement of wives' housework with purchased services. Employed wives may simply reduce their leisure time (or their sleep), or other family members may be doing more of the housework, or household standards may be lowered.

As work opportunities expand, wives' opportunity cost of not working or working part-time increases. Some of our research findings concern differences between wives' full-time or part-time employment status and family perceptions of their monetary contributions, based on family expenditures. We found indications that households perceive wives' part-time income as transitory rather than part of the family's permanent income on which lifestyle spending is based. Families with part-time working wives have an economic status more comparable to families with nonemployed wives than to those with full-time employed wives.

ECONOMIC SECURITY

At marriage, both husband and wife are employed in two-thirds of young couples, and most of these wives remain in the labor force. Increasingly, dual-earner families ensure greater economic security and provide protection to households against economic downswings and unemployment. At the macroeconomic level, they are an important factor in reducing the impact of adverse economic conditions. In the recession of the early 1980s, unemployment reached a level not seen since the 1930s, but its effects were lessened by a second worker in two-thirds of the families affected by a job loss. This provided a major cushion against the effects of unemployment on family income.

The real income of dual-earner families is increasing while one-earner family real income remains the same. The differences are even more pronounced when two-earner families are disaggregated into full-time and part-time working wives. Overall, we found pre-tax income (in constant dollars) declined for the three household types between 1972–1973 and 1986. Further, after-tax income declined for PWW an NWW families, but not for FWW families. This portends a widening income gap between full-time employed husband-wife families and other households.

There were substantial declines in mean financial assets of the three types of married-couple families between 1972–1973 and 1986, with larger decreases for FWW and NWW families than for PWW families. Assets also declined as family size increased for the three types of married-couple families.

The distribution of family income has been significantly affected by the growth of dual-earner families. As dual-earners move up in the income distribution, one-earner families fall behind, increasing the degree of income inequality. Wife's work status also affects the distribution of income, both before and after taxes, with full-time working wives increasing income equality while part-time working wives do not. As long as some wives work full-time and others part-time, the inequality of income distribution will continue to increase.

POLICY IMPLICATIONS

Income inequality due to wife's work status indicates that policies to increase equality need to facilitate full-time employment of wives. Numerous public policy implications derive from our analyses of dual-earner families. Policy measures such as tax incentives for provision of day care or broader deductions for child care costs, improved family or maternity leave policies, and the removal of tax penalties from dual-earner families will improve equality of the distribution of income. Both the federal income tax and Social Security systems incorporate negative incentives for wives' employment and favor nonworking wives. Revision of these institutional structures would remove wives' employment disincentives and increase equity toward dual-earner families.

The substantial marriage tax penalty mitigates against wives' employment. Approaches to improve tax equity and work incentives include permitting married persons to file separately, based on their own earnings and with a standard deduction allowable to each; or permitting married persons to file separately with family income shared equally. Either of these alternatives would make the individual, rather than the family, the basic unit of taxation. An alternative partial solution is reinstatement of the marriage penalty deduction.

Social Security inequities in the treatment of dual-earner families should be addressed through policy changes to eliminate the forced subsidization of one-earner families by dual-earners. An equitable approach for dual-earners would be to phase out spousal benefits, so benefits would accrue to workers, according to their contributions, approximating a compulsory pension system. Another option is to encompass nonemployed homemakers and others who opt to pay established Social Security taxes, and who can then claim retirement benefits regardless of length of marriage or marital status. Alternatively, individual Social Security taxes could be based on shared family earnings, with each spouse paying on half of total earnings. Any of these options would ameliorate current inequities in the system.

Because the present income tax and Social Security systems were instituted when one-earner households were the norm, these basic social policies discriminate against dual-earner families. Despite these institutionalized disincentives to their employment, wives continue to enter and remain in the labor force. Although changing demographics have revolutionized the American family, institutional responses have been marginal or nonexistent. The negative effects of our policies should be addressed to promote equitable treatment of different types of households.

PROJECTIONS

The growth of dual-earner families is expected to plateau during the 1990s. However, several factors indicate declines are unlikely and suggest continued growth. More families will remain intact, since the divorce rate appears to be decreasing, and these wives are likely to be employed. Younger baby boomers who have not yet married are doing so at a rapid rate and are projected to account for over 60 percent of household growth. Older baby boomers are entering their peak earning period, which is projected to increase real household income by 15 percent. This cohort of wives will maintain their strong labor force attachment, continuing to bolster household incomes. Projections for the year 2000 indicate that the number of married men earning over $50,000, in real 1990 dollars, will be almost constant, but the number of dual-earner married couples with incomes over $50,000 will increase by a third, from 18 million to more than 24 million (Baby Boomers 1992).

These demographic changes will strengthen the role and position of dual-earners among all households. Dual-earners will continue to move upward in the distribution of income, set trends in consumer goods marketing, and dominate the housing market. The real incomes of dual-earner families will continue to grow while one-earner real income remains the same or declines. Household planning and decision making will increasingly be predicated upon having two earners, which will be perceived as the norm. Dual-earner households, based on amenities, mobility, growing families, and demands for public goods, will drive private markets and public policy. The overall impact of more dual-earner families will be to stimulate and direct the economy.

Bibliography

Aaron, H. J. 1987. The impossible dream comes true. *The Brookings Review* 5(1): 3–10.

Aaron, H. J., Bosworth, B. P., and Burtless, G. T. 1989. *Can America afford to grow old? Paying for Social Security.* Washington, DC: Brookings Institution.

Abdel-Ghany, M., and Foster, A. C. 1982. Impact of income and wife's education on family consumption expenditures. *Journal of Consumer Studies and Home Economics* 6: 21–28.

Avery, R. B., and Elliehausen, G. E. 1986. Financial characteristics of high-income families. *Federal Reserve Bulletin* (March): 163–175.

Avery, R. B., Elliehausen, G. E., and Canner, G. B. 1984a. Survey of consumer finances, 1983. *Federal Reserve Bulletin* (September): 679–692.

———. 1984b. Survey of consumer finances, 1983: A second report. *Federal Reserve Bulletin* (December): 857–868.

Baby boomers are just hitting their earning stride. 1992. *Business Week* (April 6): 1:4.

Bane, M. J. 1979. Child care arrangements of working parents. *Monthly Labor Review* 102(10): 50–55.

Becker, G. S. 1965. A theory of the allocation of time. *Economic Journal* 75(299): 493–517.

———. 1988. Family economics and macro behavior. *American Economic Review* 78(1): 1–13.

———. 1991. *A treatise on the family.* Enlarged edition. Cambridge, MA: Harvard University Press.

Bell, C. S. 1976. Working wives and family income. In *Economic independence for women*, ed. J. R. Chapman, 239–261. Sage Yearbooks in Women's Policy Studies, vol. 1. Beverly Hills, CA: Sage Publications.

_____. 1981a. Demand, supply, and labor market analysis. *Journal of Economic Issues* 15(2): 423–434.

_____. 1981b. Minimum wages and personal income. In *The economics of legal minimum wages,* ed. S. Rotenberg. Washington, DC: American Enterprise Institute.

Bellante, D., and Foster, A. C. 1984. Working wives and expenditure on services. *Journal of Consumer Research* 11: 700–707.

Bergman, B. R. 1981. The economic risks of being a housewife. *American Economic Review* 71(2): 81–86. (AEA Papers and Proceedings).

_____. 1986. *The economic emergence of women.* New York: Basic Books.

Betson, D., and van der Gaag, J. 1984. Working married women and the distribution of income. *Journal of Human Resources* 19(4): 532–543.

Bird, C. 1979. *The two paycheck marriage.* New York: Wade.

Blank, R. M. 1988. Women's paid work, household income, and household well-being. In *The American woman 1988–1989: A status report,* ed. S. E. Rix, 123–161. New York: W. W. Norton.

Blau, F. D. & Ferber, M. A. 1986. *The economics of women, men, and work.* Englewood Cliffs, NJ: Prentice-Hall.

Blau, F., and Winkler, A. E. 1989. Women in the labor force: An overview. In *Women: A feminist perspective,* ed. J. Freeman. Mt. View, CA: Mayfield.

Bornstedt, G. W., and Knoke, D. 1982. *Statistics for social data analysis.* Itasca, IL: F. E. Peacock.

Boskin, M. J. 1986. *Too many promises: The uncertain future of Social Security.* Homewood, IL: Dow Jones-Irwin.

Brown, C. [Vickery]. 1987. Consumption norms, work roles, and economic growth, 1918–1980. In *Gender in the workplace,* ed. C. Brown and J. Pechman, 13–59. Washington, DC: Brookings Institution.

Brown, C., and Pechman, J. 1987. Introduction. In *Gender in the workplace,* ed. C. Brown and J. Pechman. Washington, DC: Brookings Institution.

Brown, E., ed. 1988. *Readings, issues, and questions in public finance.* Homewood, IL: Irwin.

Bryant, W. K. 1988. Durables and wives' employment yet again. *Journal of Consumer Research* 15: 37–47.

Bryant, W. K., and Zick, C. 1986. Household production, taxes, and family income distribution. *Human Ecology Forum* 15(2): 12–14.

Cain, G. G. 1967. *Married women in the labor force.* Chicago: University of Chicago Press.

Carlson, M. D. 1974. The 1972–73 Consumer Expenditure Survey. *Monthly Labor Review* 97: 16–23.

Carter, S. B. 1987. Comments on consumption norms, work roles, and economic growth, 1918–1980. In *Gender in the workplace,* ed. C. Brown and J. Pechman, 49–54. Washington, DC: Brookings Institution.

Chow, G. C. 1960. Tests of equality between subsets of coefficients in two linear regression models. *Econometrica* 28(3): 591–605.

Cochrane, W. W., and Bell, C. S. 1956. *The economics of consumption.* New York: McGraw-Hill.

Cohen, E. 1981. Commentary on family issues in taxation. In *Taxing the family,* ed. R. G. Penner, 27–30. Washington, DC: American Enterprise Institute for Public Policy Research.

Comparing child-care costs. 1992. *USA Today* (March 18): 1D.

Cooper, L. G., and Nakanishi, M. 1983. Standardizing variables in multiplicative choice models. *Journal of Consumer Research* 10: 96–108.

Cutler, B. 1989. Meet Jane Doe. *American Demographics* 11(6): 24–27, 62–63.

Danziger, S. 1980. Do working wives increase family income inequality? *Journal of Human Resources* 15(3): 444–451.

Danziger, S., Van der Gaag, J., Smolensky, E., and Taussig, M. K. 1983. The life-cycle hypothesis and the consumption behavior of the elderly. *Journal of Post Keynesian Economics* 5: 208–227.

Davis, J. S. 1945. Standards and content of living. *American Economic Review* 35(1): 1–15.

Deaton, A. 1992. *Understanding consumption.* Oxford: Oxford University Press.

DeWeese, G., and Norton, J. T. 1991. Impact of married women's employment on individual household member expenditures for clothing. *Journal of Consumer Affairs* 25(2): 235–257.

Dornbusch, R., and Fischer, S. 1981. *Macroeconomics.* New York: McGraw Hill.

Duesenberry, J. S. 1949. *Income, savings and the theory of consumer behavior.* Cambridge, MA: Harvard University Press.

England, P., and Farkas, G. 1986. *Households, employment, and gender: a social, economic and demographic view.* New York: Aldine de Gruyter.

Fareed, A. E., and Riggs, G. D. 1982. Old-young differences in consumer expenditure patterns. *The Journal of Consumer Affairs* 16(1): 152–160.

Feenberg, D. 1981. The tax treatment of married couples and the 1981 tax law. In *Taxing the family,* ed. R. G. Penner, 32–63. Washington, DC: American Enterprise Institute for Public Policy Research.

Ferber, M. A. 1983. Social and economic implications for the family of women's labor force participation. In *Proceedings of the Family Economics/Home Management Section of the American Home Economics Association,* ed. K. D. Rettig and M. Abdel-Ghany, 141–152. Madison, WI: University of Wisconsin.

Foster, A. C. 1988. Wife's employment and family expenditures. *Journal of Consumer Studies and Home Economics* 12: 15–27.

Foster, A. C., Abdel-Ghany, M., and Ferguson, C. E. 1981. Wife's employment—its influence on major family expenditures. *Journal of Consumer Studies and Home Economics* 5: 115–124.

Foster, A. C. and Rakhshani, A. 1983. The influence of wife's employment on family wealth. In *Proceedings of the Family Economics/Home Management Section of the American Home Economics Association,* ed. K. D.

Retting and M. Abdel-Ghany, 235–245. Madison, WI: University of Wisconsin.

Friedman, M. 1957. *A theory of the consumption function.* General Series, no. 63. Princeton: Princeton University Press, National Bureau of Economic Research.

Fuchs, V. R. 1986. His and hers: Gender differences in work and income, 1959–1979. *Journal of Labor Economics* 4(3): 245-272.

Fullerton, H. 1987. Labor force projections: 1986 to 2000. *Monthly Labor Review* 110(9): 19–29.

Garner, T. I. 1987. Income reporting in the U.S. Consumer Expenditure Survey. *The proceedings, American Council on Consumer Interests 33rd Annual Conference, April 1987, Denver, Colorado.* Columbia, MO: American Council on Consumer Interests.

———. 1988. Methodological issues for today and tomorrow. *Family Economics Review* 1(3): 2–5.

Gieseman, R. 1987. The Consumer Expenditure Survey: Quality control by comparative analysis. *Monthly Labor Review* 110(3): 8–14.

Gilboy, E. W. 1968. *The economics of consumption.* New York: Random House.

Guadagno, M.A.N. 1990. Family income and expenditures of married-couple families when one spouse is not employed. *Family Economics Review* 3(4): 2–11.

Hafstrom, J. L., and Dunsing, M. M. 1965. A comparison of economic choices of one-earner and two-earner families. *Journal of Marriage and Family* 27(3): 409–413.

Hamermesh, D. S., and Rees, A. 1988. *The economics of work and pay.* New York: Harper & Row.

Harrison, B. 1986. Spending patterns of older persons revealed in expenditure survey. *Monthly Labor Review* 109(10):15–22.

Hausman, J. A., and Poterba, J. M. 1987. Household behavior and the Tax Reform Act of 1986. *Journal of Economic Perspectives* 1(1): 101–119.

Hayghe, H. 1981. Husbands and wives as earners: An analysis of family data. *Monthly Labor Review* 104(2): 46–59.

———. 1983. Married couples: Work and income patterns. *Monthly Labor Review* 106(2): 26–29.

———. 1984a. Working mothers reach record number in 1984. *Monthly Labor Review* 107(2): 31–33.

———. (1984b). Married couples: Work and income patterns. *Families at work: The jobs and the pay.* U.S. Department of Labor, Bureau of Labor Statistics, Bulletin 2209 (August): 11–14. Washington, DC.

———. 1990. "Family members in the labor force." *Monthly Labor Review* 113(3): 14–19.

Hayghe, H., and Haugen, S. E. 1987. A profile of husbands in today's labor market. *Monthly Labor Review* 110(10): 12–17.

Hefferen, C. 1982. Federal income taxation and the two earner couple. *Family Economics Review* 2(Winter) 3–10.

Herz, D. E. 1988. Employment characteristics of older women, 1987. *Monthly Labor Review* 111(9): 3–12.

Horton, S. E., and Hafstrom, J. L. 1985. Income elasticities of selected consumption categories: Comparison of single female-headed and two-parent families. *Home Economics Research Journal* 13: 292–303.

Horvath, F. W. 1980. Working wives reduce inequality in distribution of family earnings. *Monthly Labor Review* 103(7): 51–52.

Jacobs, E., Shipp, S., and Brown, G. 1988. *Working wives: Do their families spend differently?* Paper presented at the American Statistical Association, New Orleans, August.

———. 1989. Families of working wives spending more on services and nondurables. *Monthly Labor Review* 112(2): 15–23.

Kakwani, N. C. 1980. *Income inequality and poverty: Methods of estimation and policy applications.* New York: World Bank Research Publication, Oxford University Press.

Kendall, M., and Stuart, A. 1977. *The advanced theory of statistics.* New York: Macmillan.

Ketkar, S. L., and Cho, W. 1982. Demographic factors and the pattern of household expenditures in the United States. *Atlantic Economic Journal* 10: 16–27.

Kossoudji, S. A., and Dresser, L. J. 1992. Gender and labor-market outcomes. *American Economic Review Papers and Proceedings* 82(2): 519–525.

Lazear, E. P., and Michael, R. T. 1980. Real income equivalence among one-earner and two-earner families. *American Economic Review* 70(2): 203–208.

———. 1986. Estimating the personal distribution of income with adjustment for within-family variation. *Journal of Labor Economics* 4(3): S216–S239.

———. 1988. *Allocation of income within the household.* Chicago: University of Chicago Press.

Leuthold, J. 1985. Work incentives and the two-earner deduction. *Public Finance Quarterly* 13(1): 63–73.

Levitan, S., Belous, R. S., and Gallo, F. 1988. *What's happening to the American family?* Rev. ed. Baltimore: Johns Hopkins University Press.

Levy, F. 1988a. *Dollars and dreams: The changing American income distribution.* New York: W. W. Norton.

———. 1988b. Incomes, families and living standards. In *American living standards: Threats and challenges,* ed. R. E. Litan, R. Z. Lawrence, and C. L. Schultze. Washington, DC: Brookings Institution.

Levy, F., and Michel, R. C. 1991. *The economic future of American families.* Washington, DC: Urban Institute Press.

Lichter, D. T., and Costanzo, J. A. 1987. How do demographic changes affect labor force participation of women? *Monthly Labor Review* 110(11): 23–25.

Linden, F. 1990. The changing face of affluence. Across the board. *The Conference Board* 27 (7,8): 9–10.

Litan, R. E., Lawrence, R. Z., and Schultze, C. L. 1988. Introduction. In *American living standards: Threats and challenges*, ed. Robert E. Litan, Robert Z. Lawrence, and Charles L. Schultze. Washington, DC: Brookings Institution.

Long, J. E., and Jones, E. B. 1980. Labor force entry and exit by married women: A longitudinal analysis. *Review of Economics and Statistics* 62(1): 1–6.

Lorenz, M. O. 1905. Methods of measuring the concentration of wealth. *Journal of the American Statistical Association* n.s. 70 (June): 209–219.

Magrabi, F. M., Chung, Y. S., Cha, S. S., and Yang, S.-J. 1991. *The economics of household consumption*. New York: Praeger.

Michael, R. T. 1985. Consequences of the rise in female labor force participation rates: Questions and probes. *Journal of Labor Economics* 3(1): S117–S146.

Minarik, J. J. 1981. Commentary on family issues in taxation. In *Taxing the family*, ed. R. G. Penner, 23–27. Washington, DC: American Enterprise Institute for Public Policy Research.

——————. 1988. *The growth and distribution of incomes in the United States*. Project Report of the Changing Domestic Priorities Project. Washington, DC: Urban Institute.

Mincer, J. 1962. Labor force participation of married women: A study of labor supply. In *Aspects of labor economics*, a report of the National Bureau of Economic Research, 63–105. Princeton: Princeton University Press.

——————. 1974. *Schooling, experience and earnings*. New York: Columbia University Press.

Nakanishi, M., and Cooper, L. G. 1974. Parameter estimation for a multiplicative competitive interaction model—least squares approach. *Journal of Marketing Research* 11: 303–311.

Nelson, J. A. 1989. Individual consumption within the household: A study of expenditures on clothing. *Journal of Consumer Affairs* 23(1): 21–41.

Nickols, S. Y., and Fox, K. O. 1983. Buying time and saving time: Strategies for managing household production. *Journal of Consumer Research* 10(3): 197–208.

Norum, P. S. 1989. Economic analysis of quarterly household expenditures on apparel. *Home Economics Research Journal* 17 (3): 228–239.

Norwood, J. L. 1984. *Working women and public policy*, 1–6. Report no. 710. Washington, DC: U.S. Department of Labor, Bureau of Labor Statistics.

Norwood, J. L., and Waldman, E. 1979. *Women in the labor force: Some new data series*. Report no. 575. Washington, DC: U.S. Department of Labor, Bureau of Labor Statistics.

O'Neill, J. 1981a. Time-series of women's labor force participation. *American Economic Review* 71(2): 76–80 (AEA Papers and Proceedings, 1980).

———. 1981b. Family issues in taxation. In *Taxing the Family*, ed. R. G. Penner, 1–22. Washington, DC: American Enterprise Institute for Public Policy Research.

Oppenheimer, V. 1970. *The female labor force in the United States*. Berkeley: Institute of International Studies, University of California.

Owen, P., and Frances, R., eds. 1980. *Dual career couples*. Beverly Hills, CA: Sage.

Pechman, J. A. 1989. *Tax reform, the rich and the poor*. Washington, DC: Brookings Institution.

Quester, A. O. 1977. The effect of the tax structure on the labor market behavior of wives. *Journal of Economics and Business* 29: 171–180.

———. 1979. Women's behavior and the tax code. *Social Science Quarterly* 59: 667–680.

Quinlan, D. C., and Shackelford, J. A. 1980. Labor force participation rates of women and rise of the two-earner family. *American Economic Review* 70(2): 209–213.

Reilly, M. D. 1982. Working wives and convenience consumption. *Journal of Consumer Research* 8: 407–418.

Reno, V. P., and Upp, M. M. 1981. Social Security and the family. In *Taxing the family*, ed. R. G. Penner, 139–164. Washington, DC: American Enterprise Institute for Public Policy Research.

Rice, D. 1979. *Dual-career marriage*. New York: Free Press.

Rosen, H. S. 1976a. Taxes in a labor supply model with joint wage-hours determination. *Econometrica* 44: 485–517.

———. 1976b. Tax illusion and the labor supply of married women. *Review of Economics and Statistics* 489: 167–172.

———. 1987. The marriage tax is down but not out. *National Tax Journal* 40(4): 567–575.

———. 1992. *Public finance*. 3rd ed. Homewood, IL: Irwin.

Rubin, R. M. 1982. Female unemployment and stagflation. *Midsouth Journal of Economics* 6(1): 1–9.

Rubin, R. M., and Gilbert, K. S. 1976. The status of women in the labor force. Paper presented at the Midsouth Academy of Economists, February.

Rubin, R. M., and Molina, D. J. 1990. Wife's work status and the distribution of income. Paper presented at the Western Economics Association, San Diego, July.

Rubin, R. M., and Riney, B. J. 1986. Second earner net income model and simulated income distributions for dual earner households. *Social Science Quarterly* 67(2): 432–441.

———. 1989. Income and asset differentials between one-earner and dual-earner households: 1972–73 and 1986. Paper presented at the Southwestern Economics Association, Little Rock, AR, March.

Rubin, R. M., Riney, B. J., and Johansen, T. 1987. Tax effects on the net income of wives in dual-earner households: 1980–1983. *Public Finance Quarterly* 15(4): 441–459.

Rubin, R. M., Riney, B. J., and Molina, D. J. 1990. Expenditure pattern differentials between one-earner and dual-earner households: 1972–1973 and 1984. *Journal of Consumer Research* 17(1): 43–53.

Ryglewicz, H. 1980. *Working couples: How to cope with two jobs and one home*. New York: Sovereign.

SAS Institute. 1985. *SAS user's guide: Basics*. Version 5. Cary, NC: SAS Institute.

Schaninger, C. M., and Allen, C. T. 1981. Wife's occupational status as a consumer behavior constraint. *Journal of Consumer Research* 8 (September): 189–196.

Schnittgrund, K. P. 1983. The influence of wife's employment on family wealth—discussion. *Proceedings of the Family Economics/Home Management Section of the American Home Economics Association*, 246–248. Madison, WI: University of Wisconsin.

Schwenk, F. N. 1989. Households with expenditures for housekeeping services, including child care. *Family Economics Review* 2(4): 15–20.

Shank, S. E. 1988. Women and the labor market: The link grows stronger. *Monthly Labor Review* 111(3): 3–8.

Shapiro, D., and Shaw, L. B. 1983. Growth in the labor force attachment of married women: Accounting for changes in the 1970s. *Southern Economic Journal* 50(2): 461–473.

Smith, J. P. 1979. The distribution of family earnings. *Journal of Political Economy* 87(5): pt. 2, S163–S192.

Soberon-Ferrer, H., and Dardis, R. 1991. Determinants of household expenditures for services. *Journal of Consumer Research* 17(March): 385-397.

Social Security: Invaluable or outmoded? 1992. *Modern Maturity* (April-May): 34–46, 84–85.

Strober, M. H. 1977. Wives' labor force behavior and family consumption patterns. *American Economic Review* 67(1): 410–417.

Strober, M. H., and Weinberg, C. B. 1977. Working wives and major family expenditures. *Journal of Consumer Research* 4: 141–147.

———. 1980. Strategies used by working and nonworking wives to reduce time pressures. *Journal of Consumer Research* 6(4): 338–348.

Sweet, J. A. 1980. The employment of wives and the inequality of family income. In *The economics of women and work*, ed. A. H. Amsden, 400–409. New York: St. Martin's Press.

Thomas, W. V. 1979. Two-income families. In *America in the 1980's*, ed. H. H. Grimlin, 73. Washington DC: Congressional Quarterly.

Thurow, L. H. 1980. *The zero-sum society*. New York: Basic Books.

Tobin, J. 1958. Estimation of relationships for limited dependent variables. *Econometrica* 26: 24–36.

Treas, J. 1987. The effect of women's labor force participation on the distribution of income in the United States. *Annual Review of Sociology* 13: 259–288.

Upah, G. D., and Sudman, S. 1981. The Consumer Expenditure Survey: Prospects for consumer research. In *Advances in consumer research*, ed K. B. Monroe, 262–265. Provo, Utah: Brigham Young University.

Urban Institute. 1992. *National child care survey of 4,400 families.* Washington, DC: Urban Institute.

U.S. Bureau of the Census. 1950. *Statistical abstract of the United States: 1950.* Washington, DC.

_____ . 1981. *Statistical abstract of the United States: 1981.* Washington, DC.

_____ . 1987. *Statistical abstract of the United States: 1987.* Washington, DC.

_____ . 1988. *Statistical abstract of the United States: 1988.* Washington, DC.

_____ . 1990. *Statistical abstract of the United States: 1990.* Washington, DC.

_____ . 1991. *Statistical abstract of the United States: 1991.* Washington, DC.

_____ . 1992. *Statistical abstract of the United States: 1992.* Washington, DC.

U.S. Department of Commerce, Bureau of the Census. 1975. *Historical statistics of the United States: Colonial Times to 1970.* Bicentennial Edition, Part 1. Washington, DC.

_____ . 1977. *Perspectives of American husbands and wives.* Current Population Reports no. 77, Series P-23. Washington, D.C.

_____ . 1989a. *Earnings of married-couple families: 1987.* Current Population Reports no. 165, Series P-60. Washington, DC.

_____ . 1989b. *Household and family characteristics: March 1988.* Current Population Reports no. 437, Series P-20. Washington, DC.

_____ . 1990a. *Household and family characteristics: March 1990 and 1989.* Current Population Reports no. 447, Population Characteristics, Series P-20. Washington, DC.

_____ . 1990b. *Marital status and living arrangements: March 1990.* Current Population Reports no. 450, Series P-20. Washington, DC.

_____ . 1990c. *Money income of households, families, and persons in the United States: 1990.* Current Population Reports no. 174, Series P-60. Washington, DC.

U.S. Department of Labor, Bureau of Labor Statistics. 1979. *1972–73 Interview survey detailed public use tape no. 2 documentation.* Washington, DC.

_____ . 1981. *Comparison of 1972–73 and 1980–81 surveys: Appendix C.* BLS Bulletin 2225. Washington, DC.

_____ . 1983. *Handbook of labor statistics.* Bulletin 2175 (December): 98. Washington, DC.

_____ . 1984. *Earnings of workers and their families: Second quarter 1984.* USDL 84–326. Washington, DC.

_____ . 1985a. *Consumer expenditures and income.* Reprint from *Handbook of Methods*, 38–42. Bulletin 2134–1. Washington, DC.

_____ . 1985b. Unpublished tabulations from Current Population Survey, 1980 and 1983 annual averages.

_____. 1986. *1984 Interview survey detailed public use tape no. 2 documentation.* Washington, DC.

_____. 1987a. *Consumer Expenditure Survey: Quarterly data from the interview survey.* Third Quarter, Report no. 763. Washington, DC.

_____. 1987b. Consumer Expenditure Survey Results From 1985. *Bureau of Labor Statistics News* (USDL 87–399), (September 24), pp. 1–7.

_____. 1989a. *Employment in perspective: Women in the labor force.* Second Quarter, Report no. 770. Washington, DC.

_____. 1989b. *Handbook of labor statistics,* 235–256. Bulletin 2340 (August). Washington, DC.

_____. 1989c. *1986 Interview survey detailed public use tape no. 2 documentation.* Washington, DC.

_____. 1991. *Marital and family characteristics of the labor force from the March 1991 Current Population Survey.* Unpublished data. Washington, DC.

_____. 1992 *Marital and family characteristics of the labor force from the March 1992 Current Population Survey.* Unpublished data. Washington, DC.

U.S. Federal Highway Administration. 1992. *Introduction to urban travel: Forecasting models.* Washington, DC.

Veblen, T. 1899. *Theory of the leisure class.* New York: Macmillan.

Vickery, C. 1979. Women's economic contribution to the family. In *The subtle revolution,* ed. R. E. Smith. Washington, DC: Urban Institute.

Wagner, J., and Hanna, S. 1983. The effectiveness of family life cycle variables in consumer expenditure research. *Journal of Consumer Research* 10: 281–291.

Waldman, E. 1984. Labor force statistics from a family perspective. In *Families at work: The jobs and the pay,* 1–6. Washington, DC: U.S. Department of Labor, Bureau of Labor Statistics. Bulletin 2209 (August).

Waldman, E., and Jacobs, E. E. 1978. Working wives and family expenditures. In *American Statistical Association 1978 Proceedings of the Social Statistics Section,* 41–49. Washington, DC: American Statistical Association.

Waldrop, J. 1989. A lesson in home economics: Working wives and empty nesters mean that married couples spend differently. *American Demographics* 11(8): 26–30.

Weinberg, C. B., and Winer, R. S. 1983. Working wives and major family expenditures: Replication and extension. *Journal of Consumer Research* 10: 259–263.

Winegarden, C. R. 1987. Women's labor force participation and the distribution of household incomes: Evidence from cross national data. *Economica* 54(214): 223–236.

Wion, D. A. 1990. Working wives and earnings inequality among married couples, 1967–1984. *Review of Social Economy* 48(1): 18–40

Wolff, E. N. 1987. Estimates of household wealth inequality in the U.S., 1962–1983. *Review of Income and Wealth* 33(3): 231–256.

———. 1989. Trends in aggregate household wealth in the U.S., 1900–1983. *Review of Income and Wealth* 35(1): 1–28.

Yang, S.-J., and Magrabi, F. M. 1989. Expenditures for services, wife's employment, and other household characteristics. *Home Economics Research Journal* 18(2): 134–147.

Author Index

Subject Index

About the Authors

ROSE M. RUBIN is a Professor in the Economics Department at University of North Texas. She has authored many journal articles and book chapters.

BOBYE J. RINEY is Professor Emeritus in the Economics Department at University of North Texas. She has written many journal articles in her career.